Don't Get Caught
with Your
Skirt Down

Don't Get Caught with Your Skirt Down

A Practical Girl's Recession Guide

Jill Keto with Daniel Keto

ATRIA PAPERBACK

New York   London   Toronto   Sydney

ATRIA PAPERBACK
A Division of Simon & Schuster, Inc.
1230 Avenue of the Americas
New York, NY 10020

First Atria Paperback edition December 2008

ATRIA PAPERBACK and colophon are trademarks of
Simon & Schuster, Inc.

For information about special discounts for bulk purchases,
please contact Simon & Schuster Special Sales at
1-800-456-6798 or business@simonandschuster.com.

Designed by Nancy Singer

Manufactured in the United States of America

10 9 8 7 6 5 4 3 2 1

ISBN-13: 978-1-4391-4586-9
ISBN-10:   1-4391-4586-5

To our children, family, and friends, who support us
with love, humor, companionship, knowledge,
and inspiration.

☙

And to women—the backbone of
home, country, and planet.

Contents

Why I Wrote This Book

The Distraction of
Soccer Games,
Pedicures, and Perez Hilton

I t was a typical Monday—the day I haul my two pre-school-aged children to their class at the Little Gym, a place where kids enthusiastically flop about on a huge mat, doing something that resembles gymnastics. Their chipper and highly trained instructors allow us mommies to take an hourlong reprieve in the waiting room while they teach the children syrupy-named skills such as "donkey kicks," "monkey jumps," and "bunny ears." The moms love it because it delivers us an hour of sanity and gives us a chance to converse with one another, comparing notes on gripping subjects such as diapers and preschools.

This day was unlike the others, because the topic of conversation moved from soccer equipment to economics. Yes, economics. My ears perked up. "This should be interesting," I thought to myself. My husband, Dan, is a total economics geek. He simply will not shut up about it. And when his endless barrage of statistics and theories doesn't make me fall asleep, some of it actually sinks in.

One mommy-girlfriend began to lament about her financial state. Firmly planted in the upper middle class, she and her husband unexpectedly found themselves in a huge pickle. You see, they had moved into a lovely fixer-upper in a very desirable Seattle neighborhood one year earlier but had not yet sold their former home (also in a popular family neighborhood), and they now had not one but *two* big-time mortgages. They had recently knocked $100,000 off the asking price of the house for sale but still had no takers. She sat doe-eyed, explaining that she and her husband had been caught completely off guard, with absolutely no clue that they might not be able to sell their first home. She said she felt as if they had been sucker-punched by the economy. She was visibly stressed, her glazed expression broadcasting her loss of hope.

I was struck by the sympathy of the other mothers and their total agreement that none of this could have been foreseen. Well, of course they never saw it coming! The women I know are so busy they scarcely have time to floss, much less sort through economic news for nuances of what the financial future might hold. Working, raising kids, running errands, doing the laundry, cleaning the house, providing taxi services, and feeding themselves and their families are all incredibly time-intensive. Add one more task to the already endless list, and these women's sanity would bust at the seams.

The other problem is that economics is, well, unsexy. It's presented in a format that's boring, difficult to comprehend, and clearly geared toward those who possess a penis. It is scarcely funny, entertaining, or hell, even slightly interesting. Women's magazines, gossip rags, and television are designed to fit into a woman's lifestyle—they provide tasty bits of information in the form of tidy Top 10 lists, two-minute segments, and juicy pictures. Slugging through an entire issue of *The Wall Street Journal* is about as much fun as a yearlong root canal when compared to what you can learn in just thirty seconds on *E!*

Sympathy was all the other mothers could offer, as not one of them had a plausible solution to this poor mother's mess. These women, by the way, are intelligent, committed, and well educated. All have at least an undergraduate college education, if not a master's degree, and yet they had not a single suggestion among them. I realized then that there's a serious lack of understanding of basic economics, what's going on in the world today, and financial planning for a weak economy—even among smart people.

My advice to our sucker-punched friend was, "Lower your asking price again and market the house yourself heavily on craigslist, on your own website, and with flyers. Do not rely on a real estate agent to do the work for you. Do it yourself and get it done. Dump the house now before it's too late."

"Too late for what?" she asked innocently.

"Before real estate prices plummet further and you and your husband end up in a serious cash-flow crunch."

Then one of the other girlfriends chimed in, "Oh no, I've heard the real estate market is picking up. In fact, the experts are saying prices will be back where they were by this summer. And remember, it's spring. This is the season when everyone moves. People have to get into a house before the coming school year. Don't worry, your house will sell eventually."

The other mommies nodded in hopeful unison. They, too, had heard that pitch on the news touting the rebound of the local real estate market. I felt pity for these unsuspecting women, buying the media's version of what the economic future held for us instead of knowing the facts and determining their own version.

I definitely have my own theories when it comes to the economy, and they have little to do with what has been on the news. My being married to an expert in practical economic theory means that the U.S. economy is discussed at our dinner table as much as weekend plans and ballet recitals. We debate, question, pare down the copious media information, and filter it to the basics. Dan provides the data, numbers, and theories. My job is to boil down the information into simple terms and concepts, then apply them in a practical way for our family. As a result, we've made some uncommon and occasionally bold moves, such as dumping our tech stocks before the crash, selling our house at the peak of the housing market, buying gold, and learning Mandarin Chinese.

What separates Dan from many of the other economists frequently seen in the news media is that he's not an armchair quarterback. Dan's been running his own business for the last thirteen years, and it has survived and thrived during economic cycles. He's not just talking about this stuff—he's doing it and has done it. For Dan, economics is not just theory; it's information for *life*.

When it dawned on me that some of our family's decisions were unusual and perhaps ahead of the curve, I felt strongly that this book needed to be written. I hope that sharing my perspective and putting economics into terms that everyone can understand might help other women to better their own lives.

Women are the target audience for this book for many reasons. First, women make 80% of the buying decisions in all homes. Today's woman is the chief purchasing officer of her household. Second, women in increasing numbers are in charge of every aspect of their family finances, including income and investments. Single women control 100% of their financial decisions. Third, it is my impression that women are frightened by this recession, which is amplified by alarming news reports about economic problems and offering no practical solutions. In fact, it's been my experience that women are more anxious and worried about the U.S. economy than men are. When you examine the statistics, their concern is justified. Women have experienced more job losses than their male counterparts during this recession and six times the median wage reduction.[1] And historically, in times of trouble, a woman is the rock of the family. She gathers her strength and sanity and pulls everyone through the difficult times.

Your money is yours, and there is no better time than a weak economy to take control of it. Even if you find economics boring and irrelevant, it's time to understand it and embrace it. And it's my hope that this book will help you do exactly that—no boredom included!

---

1. Committee on Health, Education, Labor and Pensions, Senator Edward M. Kennedy, chairman, U.S. Senate, April 18, 2002. "Taking a Toll: The Effects of Recession on Women." kennedy.senate.gov/imo/media/doc/tak ing%20a%20toll_%20report%20on%20effects%20of%20recession%20 on%20women1.pdf.

Snippets from My Life

Highlights on the Road to "Project Recession"

1976

Age Two Showed an early affinity for the finer things in life. Had a penchant for singing opera in my crib and eating butter by the stick. Off to a good start.

1980

Age Six Employed ice cream, Hostess Ho Hos, and fried chicken as my personal therapist after my parents' divorce. Started first grade and became the fattest kid in the class. Endured six years of fat jokes and playing whipping post for my classmates. Good times.

1985

Age Eleven Fell in love with dance in all forms and started studying seriously. Dropped twenty-five pounds in one summer, only to return to school unrecognizable. Fine by me.

1988

Age Fourteen My dreams of becoming a professional dancer were destroyed as I hit a growth spurt and found myself 5'8" tall with—gasp—hips. Time to hit the books.

1992

Age Eighteen Started the mechanical engineering program at Michigan State University. Discovered that this engineering stuff was hard. Studied my butt off, only to bomb my first calculus exam miserably. Classmates around me dropped like flies. I found the smartest person in my class and negotiated free daily tutoring. Managed to whip my grade up to a 98% from 48%.

1993

Age Nineteen Landed a coveted high-paying internship at Ford Motor Company world headquarters. The only skirt wearer in the group, my testosterone-laden colleagues thought it would be funny to take me out to lunch at a Detroit strip club my first day on the job. I immediately became aware that this job required a massive sense of humor, a fake ID, and a purse full of $1 bills.

As a sophomore in college, I launched my first two businesses out of my sorority room. The first was practicing cosmetology with no license on my very brave, cash-strapped sorority sisters and boys from neighboring fraternities. The second was a less glamorous consulting business to help Ford eliminate cost redundancies.

1996

Age Twenty-one I graduated from college after a tearful plea with the teacher of a class I was failing. Suddenly I faced a big career decision: go to cosmetology school, consult at Ford for $150 an hour (which is equivalent to about $300 an hour today), or take a "real" job as an engineer with Boeing for substantially less money. With an inexplicable itch to head west, I took the job with Boeing and packed my bags for Seattle.

Discovered within one week that having a corporate job is about as much fun as jamming an ice pick into your leg. My disdain for authority got me branded as a boat rocker and general troublemaker. Unpopular with management, I was assigned redundant, remedial tasks. I proceeded to spend my days surfing the web, e-mailing jokes, socializing with coworkers, and chatting up my boyfriends on the phone. My boss reprimanded me and I was officially a "disciplinary action" case. I'm pretty sure the only reason I wasn't fired is because I was the only engineer in my group with two X chromosomes.

1999

Age Twenty-five I quit my job and launched my own jewelry business with zero experience, having never made one piece of jewelry—ever. After spending seven years involved in making cars and airplanes, how complicated could jewelry be? Seventy pages of sketches, forty ounces of pounded metal, and dozens of bloody hand injuries later, I launched my first jewelry collection.

Neiman Marcus bought it. Saks Fifth Avenue followed suit three months later. Celebrities started wearing and collecting my jewelry, unbeknownst to me. One of my necklaces ended up on the cover of *Maxim* magazine. I accidentally missed out on $1.2 million in revenues because *Maxim* didn't know how to find me, so I wasn't included in the photo credit. I drank two or three martinis and banged my head on my jeweler's bench repeatedly. Learned the hard way about the value of staying on top of PR.

Dan and I sold our tech stocks before the crash. Hey, dating an economics geek has its advantages.

2000

Age Twenty-six I married my soul mate, Dan, the only person I know who disdains authority as much as I do.

2003

Age Twenty-eight Fully domesticating ourselves, Dan and I bought a 3,000-square-foot tree house/log cabin in the foothills of the Cascade Mountains outside Seattle. Its extreme architecture, soaring views, and forest setting distracted me from the enormous god-awful chocolate brown Jacuzzi bathtub and hideous light fixtures circa 1978. We rolled up our sleeves and got ready to fix her up do-it-yourself style.

Had lunch with a girlfriend who made me aware of my ticking biological clock. Better get knocked up, girl.

2005

Age Twenty-nine Decided that the most efficient way to "do the kid thing" would be to knock two of them out all at once, in the span of fifteen months. Body proceeded to turn into a soft and lumpy baby-making/lactating machine. Brain proceeded to become soft and mushy as well. Business officially went on the back burner. Endless house renovations continued. Elbows thoroughly greased.

2006

Age Thirty-one Dan announced for the millionth time that the housing market was heading south and that there were signs the U.S. economy was starting to look very shaky. The concept finally sank into my brain. The thought of losing the profits on our hard work renovating our house made me want to puke. That and the 150-pound mountain lion napping on our front lawn (seriously) made me slightly loathe our house. We decided to put it on the market, list it "by owner," post our own website, and aggressively advertise on craigslist. Six long months of frantically picking toys up off the floor and corralling the ankle biters for house showings paid off—the house finally sold. Instead of buying another house, we decided to rent for a while and invest the profit from our house sale in a variety of areas, such as precious metals and foreign stocks.

2007

Age Thirty-two Traded in my baby-making body for a firmer, less flabby version. Dug my girly clothes and high heels out of storage. Swiped Dan's copy of Timothy Ferriss's *The 4-Hour Workweek* (see Resources), which made me painfully aware that I really missed my business and couldn't stand being without it for one minute longer. I decided to relaunch and reinvent my jewelry business around the souring economy.

2008

Age Thirty-three Learned Mandarin to help get my jewelry line into the Asian markets. Became a little jealous of how easily my three- and four-year-old children sponged up the language. Set up a mini-farm in the front yard to grow our own delicious produce.

All of these life experiences led me to the point at which I can say I'm a full-fledged "Recessionista." In this book, you'll discover how I

- Prepared my family psychologically for a potential financial storm

- Eliminated all debt from our lives—we have no mortgage, no car payments, no credit card debt

- Built a successful company that will survive internationally regardless of a recession in the U.S.

- Taught myself to speak Mandarin (Chinese)

- Took control of my weight and health

- Uniquely positioned our savings and investments to take advantage of inflation, thus protecting us against the collapsing U.S. dollar and financial markets

- Turned my family into a working family, where everyone— not just the parents—contributes in some way

- Built an organic mini-farm on our suburban front yard that requires little to no maintenance

- Built a network of friends, colleagues, and neighbors for mutual support and reliance

- Spend money in a practical, responsible way without sacrificing quality, taste, or enjoyment

- Manage to save 30% of our annual income every year

Author's Note

This book may include economic analysis. All ideas, opinions, and/or forecasts expressed or implied herein are for informational purposes only and should not be construed as a recommendation to invest, trade, and/or speculate in the markets. Any investments, trades, and/or speculations made in light of the ideas, opinions, and/or forecasts expressed or implied herein are committed at your own risk, financial or otherwise.

This book is sold with the understanding that neither the author nor the publisher is providing legal, financial, investment, or other professional advice or services. If legal advice or other expert assistance is required, the services of a competent professional should be sought.

The recommendations in this book are based on the author's experience and research, believed to be reliable and accurate, but not infallible. The examples presented in this book have been chosen solely to demonstrate given points. The reader should conduct a thorough investigation of their applicability to the reader's individual circumstances.

Without personal knowledge of the reader's specific personal, professional, or financial background, it is impossible to offer intelligent advice to the reader as an individual. As such, the author and publisher disclaim any liability, loss, or risk on the reader's part, personal or otherwise, that is incurred as a consequence, directly or indirectly, of the use and/or applications of any of the contents of this publication.

This book is not intended as a substitute for financial advice from a qualified professional. The intent of this book is to provide accurate general information with regard to the subject matter covered. If financial advice or other expert help is needed, the services of an appropriate financial professional should be sought.

The purpose of this book is to educate and entertain. The author and/or publisher shall have neither liability nor responsibility to any person or entity with respect to any loss or damage caused, or alleged to be caused, directly or indirectly by the information contained in this book. All information presented in the author's websites, courses, articles, and materials are protected by registered copyright. Any reproduction of this work in any way or form constitutes copyright infringement and all involved parties will be prosecuted to the fullest extent of the law.

All brand names and product names used in this book are trademarks, registered trademarks, or trade names of their respective holders.

1

Don't Panic! Prosper

Recessions Are Not Scary; Not Knowing What to Do About Them Is

What the hell is going on? The housing market is in free fall. Grocery bills are through the roof. It costs me $70 to fill up my car's gas tank. I just witnessed a gas station attendant get bawled out by a caffeine-jolted, stressed-out soccer dad. And is it me, or did the price of salmon just double?

Welcome to our new economy! This is not a test, and no, it's not going to go away anytime soon. It's time to hunker down, get smart, and make some decisions about the bumpy road ahead. Leave your fear at the door and join me in meeting the challenges of this recession, thriving, and coming out ahead. After reading this book, you will be a full-fledged "Recessionista," capable of withstanding any challenge this recession throws your way.

But Economics Is Boring!

Yes, indeed, for most people, economics ranks up there with watching paint dry. But voluntary ignorance of it would be like not knowing how you get pregnant. *Not* smart. In either scenario, you end up frazzled and sleep deprived, with a crippling addiction to peanut butter.

Why You Need to Brush Up on Boring Economics

- We could be headed into a situation worse than the Great Depression.

- Your expenses will be going up as inflation does. Don't like last week's $200 grocery bill? How about $1,000 per week? Yes, it can happen.

- Those who are unaware or ignorant of the impending economic collapse will likely face a huge downgrade in lifestyle. Think SoHo to HoBo.

- Those who inform themselves, plan, and adapt have an excellent chance of maintaining or improving their standard of living, avoiding loss of wealth, and even increasing their wealth.

Your Man Is Not Your Financial Plan

Ladies, even if the man in your life (your husband, dad, boyfriend, brother, or boy toy) is rich, kind, and generous, you cannot assume that your financial destiny will be handled well. When it comes down to it, *you* are in charge of your money and your financial future. Nobody is going to take care of this for you.

- Only 52% of married people will reach their fifteenth anniversary.[1]

- Only 61.4% of divorced single mothers are awarded child support.[2]

- Of the single mothers who are awarded child support, nearly 53% do not receive the full payments that are due to them.[3]

- Estimates vary, but women typically experience a 27% to 45% reduction in standard of living, and sometimes poverty, immediately following divorce; whereas men increase their standard of living by up to 15% following divorce.[4]

Now, before you start squawking about how you and Mr. Wonderful will be married forever, consider the following:

- The average widow outlives her spouse by fourteen years.[5]

- 80% of women outlive their spouses.[6]

---

1. Divorce Magazine, "U.S. Divorce Statistics." www.divorcemag.com/statistics/stats.us.shtml.
2. Timothy S. Grall, "Custodial Mothers and Fathers and Their Child Support: 2005." U.S. Dept. of Commerce, www.census.gov/prod/2007pubs/p60–234.pdf.
3. Ibid.
4. Georgette Mosbacher, It Takes Money, Honey (New York: Harper Collins, 1999), 3.
5. Kathleen McCarry, University of California, and Robert F. Schoeni, University of Michigan, "Widow Poverty and Out-of-Pocket Medical Expenditures at the End of Life," California Center of Population Research, UCLA. www.ccpr.ucla.edu/ccprwpseries/ccpr_022_03.pdf.
6. Ibid.

- The average age of a widow is 56.[7]

- Widows are three times more likely to live in poverty than married women of the same age. And most (80%) of the impoverished women were not living in poverty when their husband was alive.[8]

Make no mistake about it—money is critical to your well-being. Cash might be cold comfort during tumultuous times, but it's certainly better than zero comfort. Money plays a crucial role in having a great life and achieving your goals.

THIS RECESSION IS HITTING WOMEN HARDER THAN MEN

Unemployment since March 2007 has gone up more rapidly for women than for men. In the same period, women have seen a sixfold wage decrease as compared to men and are 32% more likely to have a subprime mortgage, thus putting women at a disproportionately higher risk of foreclosure. To add insult to injury, women still earn only 77 cents for every dollar a man makes, and have significantly less in savings to fall back on.[9]

YOUR FINANCIAL ADVISER IS NOT AN ECONOMIST

Recessions arrive with their own rules affecting your money. Don't expect your financial adviser to be an economist. They

---

7. CBS News, "Financial Tips for Widows." www.cbsnews.com/stories/2003/08/13/earlyshow/living/money/printable568117.shtml.
8. McCarry and Schoeni.
9. Committee on Health, Education, Labor and Pensions, "Taking a Toll: The Effects of Recession on Women."

are two very different things. You don't expect your gardener also to be your hairstylist, right?

Keep in mind that financial advisers are the street peddlers of money market accounts, mutual funds, and retirement accounts. They get paid regardless of what the economy is doing, so they'll do exactly what they've always done. They will undoubtedly advise you to follow the same rules they always preach: diversify and sit tight, because the market "always rebounds." As you watch your net worth wither away, they'll be touting the same story, patting your hand, and telling you that everything will be all right.

Do the "Big-time" Insiders Know Something We Don't?

Since 2006, the inside players on the U.S. economy and political scene (for example, George Soros, Dick Cheney, and Jim Rogers) have been investing their assets overseas and removing/selling assets tied to the United States. They saw the writing on the wall and they don't want their wealth to evaporate. Even George W. Bush bought a 100,000-acre ranch in Paraguay. Of course, Paraguay doesn't have an extradition treaty with the U.S. . . . hmmm.

Food for Thought for Recession Doubters

Are you one of those doubters who believe that America is not already in, or going into, a recession? On the surface, it might not seem as if we are in any serious trouble yet. But take a lesson from history—the stock market crashed in 1929, but Main Street didn't feel the full wrath of the Great Depression until 1931. Right now, the canaries in the coal mine are dying. As of October 2008:

- U.S. home prices are down 19.5% from peak and still falling (the U.S. real estate market peaked in 1927 prior to the Great Depression).

- U.S. auto sales are down 40% in one year (Ford and GM are on bankruptcy watch).

- Inflation is at a thirty-year high.

- U.S. dollar value is collapsing.

- Unemployment is at a seven-year high and up 159,000 lost jobs in September 2008 alone.

- Personal bankruptcies are at record highs.

- Home foreclosures are at record highs, and rising.

- Several international banks are warning their clients of a U.S. market collapse.

- Freddie Mac and Fannie Mae, the underpinning of more than 50% of the U.S. mortgage market, have been taken over by the government.

- Lehman Brothers filed for bankruptcy and Wachovia and Washington Mutual were forced to be acquired for pennies.

- Foreign retailers are refusing to accept U.S. dollars.

- The Dow Jones is down more than 25% from its October 2007 peak.

The Silver Lining

Being aware of the rules of the recession and planning accordingly might mean the difference between barely making it and thriving. Erasing your debt and growing your wealth during a weak economy can even set you up for major wealth later on, once the storm has passed. Yes, it's true, you might be financially better off *after* a major recession or depression than you are *now*.

So join us in implementing practical steps to protecting yourself and even coming out ahead—some cases, *way* ahead.

2

Econ 101

Hold on to Your Skirts, There's an Economic Shitstorm on the Horizon

Turbulence is life force. It is opportunity.
Let's love turbulence and use it for change.
—Ramsay Clark

Why should you care about understanding economics and finance? Economics is the undercurrent that touches almost everything in our daily lives. It dictates political policy, food and gas prices, housing prices, and our ability to retire. Unfortunately, it's also been made overly complicated and difficult to understand. I will attempt to cut through the econ lingo and rhetoric and present the basics in a user-friendly way. First, we'll explore the good, the bad, and the ugly of the U.S. economy today. This will help you understand what's really going on, what to expect, and what you can do about it. That's the first step to thriving in a recession.

Business is not "as usual." We are going through a time of great change. The baby boomers are getting ready to retire, oil is becoming scarce, home values are declining, and the U.S. is involved in a never-ending war. The good news is that change always brings with it a lot of opportunity, and there will be a lot of both in the coming years.

WALL STREET AND THE GREAT CREDIT DEBACLE

Why does Wall Street matter to you? Do you own stocks? Do you have a 401(k)? Do you have a mortgage, car loans, or credit cards? Do you have money in a bank? If so, what happens on Wall Street directly affects you. Almost any financial transaction is affected by Wall Street in one way or another.

The first thing to understand about Wall Street businesses is that they do not have your best interests at heart. Like any for-profit business, they are driven to create profits for themselves, and they recognize that you and your money are a vehicle for those profits. Whether your investments succeed or fail is generally not relevant to them, because they make their money from the transaction rather than your success.

It works like this. The entire Wall Street money machine is transaction based. The firms collect a fee for every stock purchased or sold, regardless of whether it goes up or down. In the 1990s, they were peddling dot-com stocks and taking a percentage commission on every stock they sold. They made billions. In this decade, the hot seller was mortgage-backed securities and other fancy debt products. Again, they were making money with every transaction.

The trouble with following the herd is that
you inevitably step in what it leaves behind.

Wall Street tends to operate with a herd mentality, fueled by either greed or fear—or both. A good portion of Wall Street firms had their hands in the mortgage securities cookie jar because they didn't want to miss out on all the profits. There are definitely some very smart people working on Wall Street, but they are few and far between. The majority follow the party line and are just aggressive pitchmen. Still, we blindly trust them with billions and put our money where they tell us to.

Wall Street makes its money by spinning transactions such as mergers, IPOs (initial public offerings), debt securities, or stock trading. Wall Street usually wins, regardless of whether or not the investment succeeds, because they get a percentage of every transaction. In some cases even more profit can be made on a financial failure because the Wall Street insiders are on the other side (the winning side) of the losing trade. In other words, as Main Streeters are losing their shirts, some on Wall Street are making a killing. As an example, Goldman Sachs profited handsomely from the collapse of the mortgage-backed security market.

During this decade (1998–2008), Wall Street had a great time making tons of money, often at our expense. In 2007, the top twenty-five hedge fund managers made more money than all the Fortune 500 CEOs combined. When you consider that the average Fortune 500 CEO makes 400 times the average U.S. wage, that tells you where we stand relative to the hedge fund club. How did they do it? They borrowed large sums of money at very low interest rates from Japan (this is called the "carry trade"), and then used that money to buy even larger amounts of various debt products, "leveraging" themselves at 30 to 1 or higher. That means that for every $1 of assets they owned, they could borrow up to $30. That's like a bank allowing you to borrow $9 million against your home, even though it's worth only $300,000!

As long as the hedge funds were right about the direction of the market, they essentially printed cash. Unfortunately, this great Ponzi scheme has unwound and created a massive credit crisis. If you've been listening to the news lately, then you've probably heard the terms *subprime mortgage* and *CDOs* (collateralized debt obligations). These are the debt products many of these funds invested in that supposedly provided low-risk, solid returns.

Let's say you're born into "the lucky sperm club"—someone gives you $100 million. You then borrow $900 million from Japan against that $100 million, at 1% interest or less.[1] Then you buy mortgage-backed securities that might pay you 8% interest. That 8% makes you $80 million a year (8% of $1 billion), and costs you $9 million in interest (1% on $900 million borrowed). So you (the hedge fund) net $71 million in profit for the year. The hedge fund manager gets 20% of that, so he (or she? Hah!) clears more than $14 million. Not a bad job if you can get it. Especially because this club generally doesn't play with just $100 million but rather several billion. And they're not leveraged at 9 to 1 but at 30 to 1.

Alas, the game of musical chairs has ended and there aren't enough seats for everyone's big butts. Those CDOs that everyone thought were worth the $1 billion they paid for them might now be worth only 50 cents on the dollar, or even much less. If you had $100 million in investment capital and you borrowed $900 million more to buy $1 billion worth of this

---

1. Over the last decade, Japan has had historically low interest rates. The Japanese central bank cut interest rates to almost 0%. Foreign investment firms would borrow the money from Japan at very low interest rates and then invest that money in areas that achieved higher returns. The term for this is the "carry trade."

subprime junk (which is actually only worth $500 million now), then you just lost $500 million, but only $100 million was put up by investors. So you now owe $400 million more than you have.

The worst part is that all these big, distinguished banks have no way to measure accurately the real value of the CDOs that they hold. Why? Because the companies that originated the mortgages (the underlying debt product in the CDO) often misrepresented the value of the home and the creditworthiness of the borrower. CDOs are valued in $100 million increments, which means that each CDO unit can easily represent 5,000 homes. With the real estate market in free fall, it's almost impossible to determine the true underlying value of those 5,000 or more homes, and thus the value of the CDO.

In late February 2008, Goldman Sachs estimated total banking losses to be $400 billion. On March 26, 2008, Reuters reported that Goldman Sachs's credit losses totaled $1.2 trillion. That's trillion with a great big **T.** That's more money than the entire history of profits of the U.S. banking system—quick, someone run to Costco and buy a jumbo tub of ibuprofen!

In June of 2008, *The New York Times* reported that since July 2007 almost half of the profits on Wall Street had vanished—a staggering reality, considering that the period between 2004 and 2007 signified the biggest wealth boom in the history of Wall Street. The big banks involved, including JPMorgan Chase, Bank of America, Merrill Lynch, Morgan Stanley, Goldman Sachs, and Citigroup, were forced to "write down" their assets—reevaluate their worth to a price below what they paid for them—dramatically, which gutted their earnings and stock value. The game of funny numbers and fancy mortgage investments was over. As of October 1, 2008, there are no longer any stand-alone investment banks in the United States. In six months, an entire industry had vaporized. Lehman Brothers went bankrupt, Bear Stearns was eaten by JPMorgan Chase, and the two firms left standing, Morgan Stanley and Goldman Sachs, have been reorganized into commercial banks.

On September 7, 2008, the unthinkable happened. Fannie Mae and Freddie Mac, the government-sponsored corporations that fund the majority of all mortgages in the United States, were basically taken over by the U.S. government and are scheduled to be shut down over the next five years. How did this happen? In 1999, these two companies were strongly "encouraged" by politicians to expand their lending practices so that more disadvantaged persons could purchase homes. This action thrust Fannie and Freddie right into the "subprime" market and caused a massive explosion in lending activity. (See page 85 if you're not clear what *subprime* means.) As early as 2004, an auditing committee during a congressional hearing warned our not-so-bright congressmen of the potential crisis that these two companies might face because of lax underwriting practices. Fannie and Freddie, at the time, were among the largest contributors to congressional campaigns and had an army of lobbyists working the halls of Congress, so the concerns fell on deaf ears and nothing was done. Since 2006, neither company was able to report an accurate income statement or balance sheet for the Congressional Budget Office, but they were able to report record profits so management could receive millions in compensation. The music has finally stopped, and the parties dancing now realize all the chairs are gone!

The result of this absurd decadence and greed is that most of Wall Street and the global financial system is frozen with fear and doesn't know what to do. They're afraid to lend to each other because they don't trust each other anymore.

Since few banks are willing to buy packaged loans ($100 million bundles of mortgages), very few banks are willing to lend money for businesses or home mortgages because they cannot find anyone to purchase the packaged loans. This makes getting financing to buy a home or fund a business much more difficult and adds to the woes of the housing market and the overall economy.

The credit crisis affects businesses at every level, from mom-and-pop home-based businesses to the big hedge funds, and everything in-between. A March 26 bloomberg.com article illustrated this well, pointing out how small businesses like Monica Tomasso's Health e-Lunch Kids are victims of the credit crunch. Tomasso pays 35% interest on credit cards to keep her school lunch business going. For small-businesses like Tomasso's, credit is drying up. Lenders are clamping down as they themselves face staggering losses.

This credit crisis has a long way to go. According to Satyajit Das, one of the world's preeminent experts on derivatives, we are "still in the middle of the national anthem before a game destined to go into extra innings" (from "Are We Headed for an Epic Bear Market," Jon Markman, MSN Money, 9/20/2007). And this crisis is not unique to the United States, either; it has spread globally. It's possible the losses could exceed several trillion dollars when this is over. (We go into this more when we look at the bailout in the next section.) And there will likely be several more large banks that end up going out of business as Bear Stearns, Northern Rock UK, and IndyMac did.

What this means for us is that businesses will have to tighten their belts by laying off employees and cutting other expenses. It will continue to be very difficult to borrow money, and those who are able to get loans will pay more for them. Life for many will be very challenging.

JUICY BITS

The global financial system runs on credit (money). Wall Street's greed, fueled by excessive and easy credit from the central banks, created the investment bubble that has inflated the real estate market and many stocks. This bubble now has a huge hole in it and is deflating rapidly. We are still in the early stages of this crisis. Business and daily life will become much more challenging as the losses, created by excess, grow.

THE AMAZING BAILOUT BOONDOGGLE

The "bailout" plan is just a perpetuation of the debt addiction of the United States. Prior to the Federal Reserve Act of 1913, money was actually backed by assets. After the Federal Reserve Act was passed, our monetary system slowly transitioned from a currency backed by the assets of the United States to a currency backed by debt. That debt is in the form of U.S. Treasury bonds, which are backed by future earnings of American taxpayers. There began the culture of debt in our society. The concept of paying with cash has, until very recently, been considered passé. Average consumers were encouraged not to worry about what they could afford to buy with cash, but what they could afford to buy in monthly installments. On every level, our system has adopted this culture of debt and instant gratification. State and local governments, the federal government, businesses, and the vast majority of society buy now and pay later. Instead of dealing with intense pain that would last a year and then reconverting our culture and monetary system to one based on assets, the powers that be chose the easy path creating more debt and printing more money. The bailout will result in a much longer and deeper recession than if they had just let the system correct itself.

Passed and signed into law on October 3, 2008, the bailout is the largest transfer of wealth in the history of the United States. What started as a three-page document giving Treasury Secretary Henry ("Hank") Paulson $700 billion and dictatorial powers over the U.S. economy turned into a 450-page document and more than $850 billion. This bailout does little for Main Street. The true cost, economist and investment adviser Marc Faber told Bloomberg News in an interview, is closer to $5 TRILLION. So who benefits from this? Wall Street. The bailout has the U.S. Treasury buying up all the toxic assets on the books of Wall Street banks. This is great for the banks. They get to clean up their books and resume the huge bonuses Wall Street is famous for. The problem is, all this toxic junk is now owned by the U.S. Treasury and, by default, the U.S. taxpayer. Yep, that's right, we the people once again get to pay for the mess of Wall Street. Hank Paulson used to be the CEO of Goldman Sachs (and is worth over $500 million), so he is just taking care of his own.

Wall Street and our mentally challenged elected officials in D.C. are blaming the subprime mortgage fiasco for this problem. I would like to put this in perspective. Let's assume that there are 3 million homes in foreclosure or about to go into foreclosure and that the average mortgage debt on these homes is $150,000. Do you realize that $450 billion would pay off the *entire mortgage* on *all* of these homes! If we just wanted to bring these mortgages current, the cost would probably be no more than $100 billion. So why do we need to obligate the U.S. taxpayer to trillions in obligations? Because the big players on Wall Street, in their great wisdom and desire for profits, decided to borrow trillions against these mortgage-backed securities and create a $600 trillion "derivative" bubble.[2] This bubble is now deflating. With a $600 trillion financial bomb going off, do you really believe the government will stop with a measly $700 billion on this bailout? Welcome to hyperinflation and the collapse of the U.S. dollar.

The Dollar, and Other Fun Things to Wipe Your Butt With

The U.S. dollar is competing with Charmin for the honor of being the world's most popular toilet paper. The U.S. Federal Reserve (the bank that prints the U.S. dollars), over the last few decades, has run the printing presses overtime, flooding the world with greenbacks. Perhaps the rest of the world is wising up, because since 2001, the value of the dollar has dropped precipitously. A dollar used to be worth over 1.2 euros and now is worth only 0.6 euros. Take a vacation to France; you will quickly learn where our currency stands in the world. Forty dollars for some "freedom fries," anyone? Even in India, they would rather be paid in rupees than dollars.

The Federal Reserve Chairman, Ben Bernanke, is nicknamed Helicopter Ben for his famous speech about how the Federal Reserve has a secret weapon called the printing press, and that they will rain money down from helicopters if they have to. So far, he has lived up to his nickname and continues to print money with reckless abandon. The rest of the world has lost faith in the dollar and in the Bush Administration's endless war(s), and is tired of America's record trade deficit. How are they responding? By dumping dollars in favor of the

---

2. I have read studies that state the actual total outstanding derivatives are now over $1.2 quadrillion. That is 1.2 million billion!

euro and other currencies. What does this mean? Stuff that the U.S. imports has become, and will continue to be, much more expensive. What do we import? Pretty much everything now. Just go to Wal-Mart and read the "Made in" label on any product.

Inflation: What It Is, and Why a Martini Costs $30

When prices go up, it's called inflation. If you listen to the government bureaucrats, inflation is completely under control. If you believe that, I have a bridge to sell you. Anyone who has gone grocery shopping lately knows that food prices are skyrocketing. However, according to U.S. government data, inflation has been running between 2% and 3% in recent years. The reality is that inflation is actually running between 8% and 12%. Why the disparity?

Let's look at how *they* calculate inflation. First, they like to exclude the "volatile" food and energy sectors. Instead, they focus predominantly on manufactured goods and services. Then, to make their system even more difficult to decipher, the government incorporates product "quality adjustments" and "product substitution" into their calculations. A quality adjustment for a new-model laptop computer, for example, would account for the fact that it is ten times faster than one produced five years ago but costs the same. Instead of the inflation on that product being calculated at 0, it's actually given a negative number because the product is ten times faster. "Product substitution" is even more creative. The government assumes that if a product moves up dramatically in price, the consumer will just buy a cheaper, similar product; thus, the product really didn't go up in price. Based on that argument, I guess if we all just eat dog food, that will solve our inflation woes. The last factor that discounts inflation is housing. The government economists look at rental costs rather than home prices. During the last six years, though home prices were climbing sky high, rents were held down because easy-money "teaser" mortgages often made it cheaper to buy an overpriced home than to rent something similar. Thus, rental rates stayed constant and the government claimed there was no housing inflation!

According to government mathematicians inflation has consistently remained between 1% and 3% for the last decade or so. But their deliberately misleading way of calculating inflation has invited some major tomato throwing. Financial manager and investment author Bill Gross believes that the U.S. Bureau of Labor Statistics method for calculating inflation underreports true inflation. The rest of the world's inflation has averaged nearly 7% over the last decade, but the official U.S. rate has averaged 2.6%. Mr. Gross questions whether it makes any sense that our inflation rate is 3% to 4% lower than the rest of the world's. The short answer is no.

There is a logical reason why the government does this, and it's not just a hopeless attempt to make the administration seem slightly more palatable to the average voter. Rather, government employee wages, pensions, Social Security, and many other programs are indexed to inflation. If the government reported true inflation numbers, its expenditures would grow even faster because it would have to give its employees raises to keep up with inflation. Therefore, there is an inherent incentive on the government's part to downgrade the inflation numbers. Hey, government employees want to keep their jobs just like the rest of us.

Real inflation has been between 7% and 12% these last six years, and is accelerating. Gold in 2001 was $270 an ounce and in March 2008 broke $1,000 an ounce. In 1998 oil was

$12 a barrel, and in May 2008 it hit $135 a barrel. Wheat was
$3.50 a bushel in 2004 and $13 a bushel in March 2008. Pretty
much every commodity, the stuff that goes into everything we
buy, is at record highs, and it doesn't look as if the increases
will end anytime soon.

As the following graph shows, the dollar has lost almost
90% of its value since 1950.

GRANDFATHER ECONOMIC REPORT,
HTTP://MWHODGES.HOME.ATT.NET/

INFLATION: 89% DECLINE IN
PURCHASING POWER OF THE DOLLAR
(A 1950 DOLLAR NOW WORTH 11.5 CENTS)

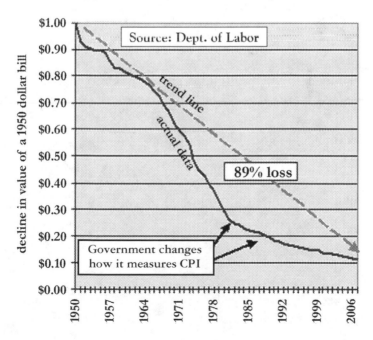

Here are some basic examples:

- A postage stamp in the 1950s cost 3 cents; today's cost is 42 cents—1,300% inflation

- A gallon of 90 octane gasoline cost 18 cents in 1955 (and you got full service); now $3.65 for self-service—2,000% inflation

- A house in 1959 cost $14,100; today's median price is $213,000—1,400% inflation

- A dental crown in the 1950s cost $40; today it's $1,100—2,750% inflation

- An ice cream cone in 1950 cost 5 cents; today it's $2.50—4,900% inflation

- Monthly Medicare insurance premiums cost seniors $5.30 in 1970; now they cost $93.50—1,664% inflation (and up 70% in the past five years)

Look at what happened to food prices just between 2007 and 2008, and yet the government insists inflation is moderate.

Food Item	Unit	May 2007	May 2008	Change
Chuck, GROUND	Pound	$2.766	$2.798	1.16%
Beef, Ground	Pound	$2.307	$2.313	0.26%
Steak, Round Choice	Pound	$4.134	$4.178	1.06%

TURKEY, FROZEN	Pound	$1.146	$1.258	9.77%
EGGS, GRADE A	Dozen	$1.504	$1.93	28.32%
MILK	Gallon	$3.259	$3.76	15.37%
CHEESE, CHEDDAR	Pound	$3.976	$4.397	10.59%
BARLEY	Bushel	$3.12	$4.76	52.56%
BEANS, DRY	100 pounds	$3.08	$5.06	64.29%
CORN	Bushel	$3.49	$5.12	46.70%
COTTON	Pound	$0.44	$0.61	37.95%
FLAXSEED	Bushel	$7.08	$16.60	134.46%
LENTILS	100 pounds	$13.20	$32.70	147.73%
OATS	Bushel	$2.49	$3.46	38.96%
POTATOES	100 pounds	$7.95	$9.21	15.85%
RICE, ROUGH	100 pounds	$10.00	$15.00	50.00%
SOYBEANS	Bushel	$7.12	$12.30	72.75%
WHEAT	Bushel	$4.88	$8.80	80.33%
APPLES	Pound	$0.27	$0.34	26.02%
GRAPEFRUIT	Box	$4.49	$5.12	14.03%
LEMONS	Box	$8.14	$20.77	155.16%

PEACHES	Ton	$820.00	$948.00	15.61%
ASPARAGUS	100 pounds	$91.90	$99.80	8.60%
BROCCOLI	100 pounds	$26.70	$27.30	2.25%
CAULIFLOWER	100 pounds	$24.90	$37.40	50.20%
CELERY	100 pounds	$18.30	$37.70	106.01%
LETTUCE	100 pounds	$13.60	$16.80	23.53%
ONIONS	100 pounds	$24.20	$31.70	30.99%
SNAP BEANS	100 pounds	$38.80	$39.60	2.06%
SWEET CORN	100 pounds	$21.40	$23.10	7.94%
TOMATOES	100 pounds	$35.60	$40.40	13.48%

Sources: United States Department of Agriculture (USDA): National Agricultural Statistics Service (NASS) and Economic Research Service (ERS).

Inflation is a global problem as well. On March 24, 2008, Bloomberg News reported that consumer price inflation in Russia had increased to an annual rate of 12.7%. Every country is feeling the pain, and the poorer nations—those least able to afford increases in food and energy—are suffering the most.

𝒥UICY BITS

Everyday life in America, and the rest of the world for that matter, is going to get a lot more expensive. It's crucial to know how to protect yourself from inflation to help you maintain your current lifestyle.

ASSET DEFLATION

What goes up must come down. Often, inflation collapses into deflation, when prices decline. Many asset classes experienced strong inflation this last decade due to excessive money created by the global central banking system. As we've discussed, many of these assets were bought with large amounts of debt. As a general rule, an asset class purchased primarily with debt has a high probability of a strong price decline. An obvious example of this is the residential real estate market. Over the last six years, the United States and most of the world experienced an incredible increase in housing prices. In America, the banking establishment was practically standing on street corners giving away home loans to anyone with a pulse, and quite possibly a few people without. What a deal—on an income of $20,000 per year, you could buy a $600,000 home with no money down and a six-month teaser loan payment of $1,000 a month! The real estate industry convinced everyone that house values grow at 20% a year and never go down. How can you lose? Sign me up!

People began to think of their homes not as a place to hang their hat but as a way to get rich. A house became one's giant ATM machine, ready to spit out cash in the blink of an eye with a quickie refinancing. Gotta have that shiny new Hummer!

BLINDED BY THE BLING

A lot of people bought into the dream of the ever-appreciating housing market. And guess what? House values don't always go up. In fact, they can come down faster than they rise, which is what's happening right now. All those cheap teaser loans are rolling over, house prices are crashing, and foreclosure rates are at historic highs. Many properties are so far "underwater"— meaning their current market value is lower than their mortgage balance—their owners are sending the house keys to their lenders (the banking industry calls this "jingle mail") and walking away from their homes, sometimes taking the copper wiring with them.

The easy loans created excessive demand, and home builders went on a building rampage. It's fascinating how those in the building industry never thought it would stop. The CEO of Toll Brothers, one of the biggest U.S. home-building companies, went on record in late 2005 (*USA Today*) and stated that the housing market would "absolutely" be fine for years to come.

The beginning of the end arrived nine months later, and the proverbial shit has now hit the fan. Unfortunately, because of the lead time involved with new construction, these builders are still pumping out inventory in 2008. There are so many unsold homes on the market that it will be many years before the nation's home inventory reaches normal levels. This does not bode well for housing prices.

Let's be clear about something here: a home is not an investment; it is where you live and needs to be looked at as such. Historically, true housing investment returns barely outpace inflation. Don't get me wrong—there are times when homes are a great investment, and we will get into that later. But right now is not a great time to buy a home.

The next big shoe to drop will be commercial real estate. It also experienced an unprecedented building boom. As the economy slows, overleveraged builders will go bankrupt and leave many projects unfinished. This has already happened in Las Vegas and other parts of the country. As demand for space diminishes, commercial land prices will experience sharp declines.

The U.S. stock market is also experiencing strong sector deflation. All business sectors that were dependent on the easy credit of the last six years will suffer greatly from this credit crisis.

𝒥UICY BITS

Most of the banking, auto, housing, consumer credit, and retail sectors will continue to struggle. Because they are so dependent on access to easy credit, the credit crisis will continue to create strong deflationary trends for them. There may still be individual companies within those sectors that do very well, but as an aggregate, they should continue to deflate.

MEDIA

Be very wary of what you hear from the "financial experts" on television. According to an academic study conducted in the late 1990s, approximately 75% of money managers underperform the major stock indices. Even the picks of CNBC's venerable loudmouth Jim Cramer have underperformed the market in the last few years. Realize that most of the television experts are there to market their funds or are being paid to tell a story. You seldom, if ever, see the real gurus like Warren Buffet, Bill Gross, or George Soros on these programs.

Drew Curtis's brilliant *It's Not News, It's Fark: How Mass Media Tries to Pass Off Crap as News* (2007) exposes the inner workings of the media machine, its tendency to spread misinformation, and its bias. And it's great bathroom reading; it will make you laugh until you pee.

COST-OF-LIVING INFLATION + DEFLATING ASSETS = STAGFLATION

Although "stagflation" sounds benign, it will devastate the American middle class. I don't like the term because it's misleading. It sounds like "stagnant," which evokes a neutered, watered-down message. But in fact, stagflation is a very, very serious issue. Using the term *stagflation* is very smart political spin. As far as political media is concerned, it serves as a clever substitute for a scary word: *recession*.

But you can take positive steps, prepare for change, and thrive. The first and most important step is to eliminate debt.

NATIONAL DEBT

I place economy among the first and most important virtues, and debt as the greatest of dangers to be feared.

—Thomas Jefferson

As a country and as a people we are in debt up to our ears, and our friendly neighborhood loan shark, Guido, is standing at the door. The United States has been living way beyond its means during the last couple of decades, and if we're not careful, it'll soon be thumb-breaking time.

For a simple analogy, let's say you go get ten credit cards with $10,000 limits. You can live pretty well for a year or two with that additional credit. However, eventually you'll have to pay your bills or go bankrupt. On a very large scale, the U.S. government, U.S. businesses, and much of the U.S. population have been borrowing trillions to fund their current lifestyles. The rest of the world has been our lender. How do they lend? By buying U.S. Treasury bonds or various other debt instruments peddled by Wall Street. Now they're starting to realize that we might not be able to pay them back, so they're beginning to stop lending to us.

This excerpt from an article in the March 27, 2008, issue of the *Financial Times* (with contributors Song Jung-a, Seoul; Andrew Wood, Hong Kong; and Michael MacKenzie, New York) highlights our troubles to come: "The world's fifth-largest pension fund said yesterday it would no longer buy U.S. Treasuries because yields were too low, signaling what could be a big shift by financial institutions away from U.S. government debt into higher yielding assets."

Total American debt is now $53 trillion ($41.5 trillion in private household, business, and financial sector debt plus $11.5 in federal, state, and local government debt). This does not include future obligations of pensions, Medicare, or Social Security. Those add an additional $64 trillion to the total debt.

This is equivalent to $175,000 per person (including children), which is $700,000 per family of four. If we include several unfunded liabilities (Medicare, Social Security benefits, government employee pension plans, and a host of others), then total debt (private plus government) is *$117 trillion*, equivalent to $385,000 per person or $1.5 million per family of four. Considering that the U.S. has a GDP (gross domestic product) of $14 trillion, you have to question how this will ever be paid. We are so addicted to debt that for every dollar of growth in GDP, we need to add an additional five dollars of debt to the system.

Total American Debt versus National Income

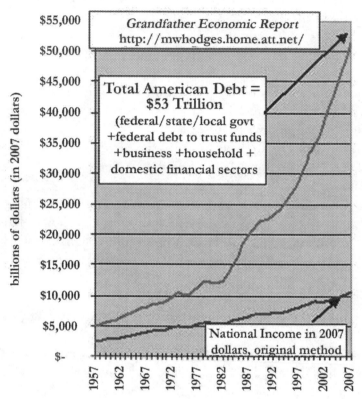

Data: Federal Reserve U.S. Treasury Bureau Economic Analysis

Why National Debt Is Bad

At one time, the U.S. owed the national debt to itself and the interest on the debt stayed in the U.S. Now our national debt is mostly held abroad. Foreign creditors collect interest on it, which results in a net drain on income for the U.S. The bill collectors are calling and someone has to pay them. Who? We the people. Get ready, for the taxman cometh!

The Boomer Bomb

The baby boomers (those born between 1946 and 1965) have redefined American culture and politics over the last fifty years. Their parents lived through the Great Depression, and then returned victorious from war to a country of infinite possibilities. Unlike their parents, who struggled through the Great Depression just trying to make ends meet, the boomers grew up with great affluence and became accustomed to prosperity. In fact, they came to expect it. The boomers elected politicians to suit their needs. Businesses thrived as credit became an acceptable and expected part of life. Financing companies, like those responsible for issuing auto loans, credit cards, and mortgages, loosened their standards to allow borrowing from nearly every one of the boomers, even the welfare recipients and drug dealers. The boomers' inherent sense of entitlement, coupled with easy credit, sparked the most massive spending spree in history.

The media frequently, and incorrectly, portrays the boomers to be wealthy, with cash reserves and lots of savings. Wrong. In fact, boomers have been crippled by their out-of-control entitlement mentality, pissing away their money instead of saving it. Savings? The boomers have no motivation to save, what with home equity and stock values increasing every year.

Their incredible numbers and purchasing power have dictated many of our current social and economic trends. The unfunded liabilities of $64 trillion discussed in the previous section are largely driven by the entitlement programs for the boomers. When Social Security was first implemented, there were eleven workers for each retiree. When the boomers retire, there will be two workers for each retiree. Also, people are now living much longer than they did fifty years ago. One has to wonder where the money for the Social Security program will come from.

There is no trust fund for Social Security and Medicare. The "fund" is an illusion; the pot is empty. The way it works is that we pay taxes. The government collects the tax money and puts it into a phony trust fund. It then pulls the money out to fund the war, or spend it wherever else it's immediately needed. The government writes an IOU to the trust fund for the money owed, but that's a bit like writing an IOU to your bank account for money you've withdrawn and still claiming that amount as an asset. Ridiculous.

The end result is that if you're a baby boomer and think you'll be able to live off your Social Security, think again. Social Security is in trouble. The government solution will be to increase taxes dramatically or reduce the entitlement programs. (They are already doing this by indexing them to the government's fictitious inflation numbers.) It will likely be a combination of both.

The boomer retirement will also have an additional depressing effect on housing. When the average person moves toward retirement, downsizing is the goal. This is typically done by selling the big house and moving to a retirement area or a smaller home or condo. As the boomers migrate out of the suburbs, the generation that will replace them (Generation X) is 30% to 40% smaller. That means there will be a lot more homes for sale than there are buyers, which will deflate prices further, though the places boomers move to may experience price inflation, or at least better stability in the current housing crisis.

Boomers will also have a big effect on the stock market. When people retire, they stop contributing to their 401(k) and instead start withdrawing money from it. The boomer retirements will reverse the flow of billions of dollars that were going into the stock market. This will likely create a scenario similar to the one in Japan over the last twenty years. In 1989, the Nikkei index hit 40,000. Nineteen years later, it's at 13,000. It is very possible that the U.S. markets will experience the same magnitude of decline. An excellent study of this demographic trend is provided by economist Harry S. Dent in *The Next Great Bubble Boom: How to Profit from the Greatest Boom in History, 2005–2009* and *Demographic Trends in Real Estate*. He also has a newsletter at www.dentadvisors.com.

If the preceding issues aren't enough, the world now has to deal with declining energy production, which leads us to . . .

Peak Oil?

When I first learned about the concept of Peak Oil, back in 2002, it pretty much freaked me out. Nobody was talking about it back then, which made it worse. Some people react to the gloomy reality of Peak Oil with full-fledged hysteria, investigating farms to buy in remote areas and planning to become hermits. This is not an option for me, as that lifestyle would seriously impede my socializing schedule, cultural exposure, and outings for Thai food.

Peak oil is also known as Hubbert's Peak. Dr. M. King Hubbert was a geophysicist who studied the life cycle of oil wells and postulated that the United States would peak its oil production in 1972. When he presented his theory (in the 1950s), he was laughed at and scorned by the oil industry because the United States was the largest oil producer in the world. Guess what happened in 1972? U.S. oil production peaked at 8 million barrels a day and has since declined to about 5 million barrels a day. You may remember the oil embargo in the 1970s, or have probably at least heard of it. Gas was rationed, prices went through the roof, and people were pretty pissed off.

The General Depletion Picture

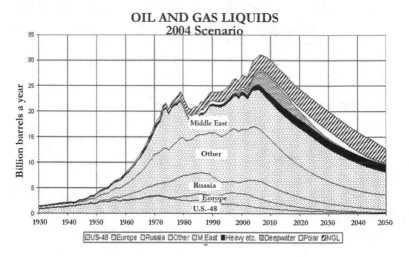

OIL AND GAS LIQUIDS
2004 Scenario

Source: ASPO (Association for the Study of Peak Oil)

Hubbert also predicted that global oil would peak around 2000. He was off by a couple of years, but many now suspect that the world hit Peak Oil in 2005 because global production has not exceeded that year's 74 million barrels a day (mbd) of crude oil. Meanwhile, daily consumption has hit 84.4 mbd, with the difference coming from drawdowns in inventories, which are dwindling, and natural gas liquids, which are also approaching a peak in production.

What does this mean? Oil touches pretty much every single thing we use, eat, consume, walk on, wear, and drive. The entire global system is centered on energy, and if energy starts to dry up, there are going to be some pretty serious consequences. The United States consumes roughly 21 mbd and imports 16 mbd, so we are very dependent on the rest of the world for our energy needs.

Now China and India are growing up, and they too want their fair share of the world's oil. Here's some basic math. Oil demand is growing several percent a year (it's currently at around 85 mbd), and oil production has flattened at around 84 mbd. Hmmm, we need 85 and we're getting 84. When this happens, prices go through the roof. Have you checked the prices at the gas pump lately? Holy $hit!

The economists in the room will tell you that when prices go up, the market responds and will invest in the drilling of more oil. This is great if oil is an unlimited resource. But since oil comes from dead dinosaurs baked into the Earth's crust for millions of years, it's not terribly likely that we'll be making any more. In fact, the United States has been drilling like crazy these last few years with very bad results.

More Drilling, Less Oil

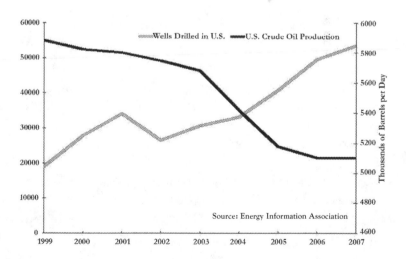

Source: Energy Information Association

Economists say that new alternatives for energy will arrive to replace oil. This is true to some extent, but the world should have been working on this issue thirty years ago. To put it in perspective, it costs $10 to pull a barrel of oil out of the ground in Iraq or Saudi Arabia. That barrel of oil creates the equivalent energy of 25,000 labor hours. That is one heck of a return on investment. There are many other energy resources, but the returns are dramatically lower, and in some cases, like ethanol, it is possible that they may even be negative. In a Cornell University News Service article published July 5, 2005, science writer Susan S. Lang cites a Cornell and University of California–Berkeley study showing that turning plants into fuel uses more energy than the resulting ethanol or biodiesel generates. This means that the transition away from fossil fuels to other energy sources will require a pretty dramatic shift in lifestyles—away from abundant consumption and toward conservation and frugality.

This is not TEOTWAWKI (the end of the world as we know it). What Peak Oil means is that things are going to change a whole lot for those of us in the United States. If you look around your town or city, you'll note that it's pretty much designed around the automobile. Most people live in suburbia and hop into their SUVs and drive a couple miles to buy milk. If Peak Oil is real, then the American lifestyle will change. Those who don't change will pay financially because the cost of transportation, and pretty much everything else, will go up substantially.

All of these wonderfully depressing issues basically lead us to the conclusion that the United State is in for one heck of a roller-coaster ride that will likely lead to a prolonged recession.

JUICY BITS

- *Expect that through inflation, everything is going to get much more expensive. Housing, though, is one area in which prices will continue to fall.*

- *The U.S. is in massive debt to the rest of the world, which we have to pay back.*

- *Stocks will be hit hard as the baby boomers retire and pull their money out of the market.*

- *Taxes are likely to go up dramatically to fund entitlement programs for the boomers.*

- *Oil production has likely peaked, meaning that gas will be even more expensive.*

RECESSION HEAT INDEX

	SMOKIN' HOT	TEPID	CHILLED
Inflation	$5 bell pepper	$5 Tee-shirt	$5 martini
National debt	Borrowing from China	Borrowing from Japan	Borrowing from Europe
Mortgage bombs	Commercial defaults	Adjustable rate rollover	Subprime crisis
Hedge fund managers	Prison sentences	Shutting down the fund	Seven-figure bonuses
Wall Street	Collecting unemployment	Liquidation of art collection	Masters of the Universe
Bankruptcy	U.S. government bankruptcy	Commercial bankruptcy	Personal bankruptcy
Currency	Got gold?	Euro	U.S. dollar
Stocks	Resource stocks	Emerging markets	U.S. stocks
Vehicle of choice	Bicycle	Prius	Hummer

3

Wake Up and Smell the Recession

Recession, Greater Depression, or a Walk in the Park?

*There is no means of avoiding the final collapse of
a boom brought about by credit (debt) expansion.
The alternative is only whether the crisis should come
sooner as the result of a voluntary abandonment of
further credit (debt) expansion, or later as a final and
total catastrophe of the currency system involved.*
                                        —Ludwig von Mises

There is no doubt as of October 2008 that the United States is in a recession. In September alone, 159,000 jobs were lost—the largest increase in unemployment in seven years. Even the most ardent economic optimists acknowledge it, and it's been pretty obvious to people on Main Street for the last six months. The $20,000 question is: will it be a short, shallow recession like ours in the early 1990s or a deep, prolonged recession like Japan's since 1989? Or, will it be the "Greater Depression," reminiscent of the 1930s?

First, some definitions. Technically, a recession is two or more quarters in a row of negative economic growth as measured by the country's Gross Domestic Product (GDP). The GDP is the sum of all goods and services a country produces, and in theory, it is supposed to continue to grow. When it stops growing and starts shrinking you are in a recession. Politicians hate this because they usually lose their election when a recession occurs. In the last forty years, we have had several recessions, most recently in 2001 and 1990–91. Recessions are considered to be part of the natural business cycle.

A really bad and prolonged recession is called a depression. The United States has not had a depression since the 1930s, the Great Depression. During depression we experience dramatic increases in unemployment, bankruptcies, unavailability of credit, and a prolonged contraction of the economy. Bottom line: They are not fun and you want to avoid them.

So the question is, what is the United States in for now? Unfortunately, my crystal ball is in the shop, so I cannot say for sure what kind of recession or depression is in store for us. I can, however, present arguments for and against each case and let the reader decide. In my humble opinion, it's always best to prepare for the worst but expect the best. That way, you won't get caught with your skirt down.

Perspective Check from the Great Depression

"No one foresaw the impending ominous future in the late 1920s, but a very few were fortunate if their timing happened to be just right.

"Leonard Lone of Augusta, Wisconsin, had worked hard and very long hours in the lumbering business, and had saved frugally. By 1928, he had $3,000 in the bank, a girlfriend named Lillian, and an urge to settle down.

"He drew out all of his money and bought a 120-acre farm for $2,000 cash. Then he bought a new 1929 Model A Ford, the classiest one on the market with a rumble seat in the back, for $675. He made his decisions just in time, because soon after, the Bank of Augusta closed. A neighbor had all his savings in there, and after the fateful morning of April 14, 1929, he had only the fifteen cents that was in his pocket.

"On November 6, 1930, Leonard and Lillian were married on his birthday. They had money left over to buy furniture for the house, and he was fortunate again in that he found employment with Eau Claire County for 75 cents an hour, and worked there throughout the entire Depression."

—*Submitted by Lillian Lone, Augusta, Wisconsin*

From *Stories and Recipes of the Great Depression of the 1930's* by Rita Van Amber (see Resources).

Scenario One: Brief, Shallow Recession

After the unprecedented sequence of financial bombs going off in September and subsequent market meltdown, most of the talking heads on the tube and the so-called financial "experts" finally agree we are in a recession, but most believe the recent bailout will keep it shallow and short. However, we are beginning to hear some "experts" claim we are headed for a depression. If you consider that they are in the business of selling stocks and good news, it is a bit shocking that they are broadcasting this message.

Arguments for a Shallow Recession

- The Fed: The Federal Reserve Bank began cutting interest rates aggressively in the last half of 2007, and so far in 2008, it has cut rates at record levels and pumped several hundred billion dollars into the banking system. Additionally, Congress just passed an unprecedented bailout package that will purchase more than $700 billion in bad-debt securities from the banking system, and the Federal Reserve injected more than $500 billion of additional money into the banks. The government is praying that these unprecedented moves will unfreeze the credit markets, lower borrowing costs, and get the economy moving again.

- The rest of the world's central banks are also buying up billions in bad debt and pumping billions more into their financial systems.

Arguments Against a Shallow Recession

- The U.S. consumer is tapped out, and this is a consumer-based recession, not a business-based one. Consumer recessions tend to run longer and deeper.

- The housing market has not bottomed yet, and foreclosures are still rising. Over the last five years, U.S. consumers were using the appreciation in their homes to supplement their wages. The price correction has reduced this access to credit. The recent bailout does nothing for the people who cannot pay their mortgages, but instead just helps the banks who hold the bad mortgages.

- The credit markets are still in complete turmoil and banks are still afraid to lend to each other and I do not think this bailout will lessen their fears. This will dampen business activity and drag out the recession.

CONSEQUENCES OF A SHALLOW RECESSION

Most people will remember the recessions of 1990–92 and 2000–02. They were small recessionary periods led by a downturn in the business cycle. Unemployment climbed, and many businesses lost money or went bankrupt. Shallow recessions are often looked at as partly positive because they weed out the weaker businesses and allow the strong ones to survive and thrive. The dot-com implosion is an excellent example. Poor ideas like Pets.com and WebVan went out of business, and great Internet businesses like Google and eBay thrived.

People who were financially on the edge got hurt, but most rebounded and learned a good lesson. Those who lived within their means probably didn't notice much change other than the somber mood of the nation.

SCENARIO TWO: DEEP, PROLONGED RECESSION

In my opinion, this is the most probable scenario. When you look in detail at the multitude of economic factors the United States is facing (see Econ 101), it's hard to believe that a short recession will cure the problem. The entire system has been on a credit binge over the last decade, and the hangover will likely be a doozy.

ARGUMENTS FOR A LONG RECESSION

- Credit crisis: The massive credit bubble is popping and there are $600 trillion of these securities/derivatives in the financial system that are difficult to value. As this credit debacle unwinds, many large banks may go out of business or need to be bailed out by the government (following the path of Northern Rock UK, Bear Stearns, Washington Mutual, Lehman Brothers, and Wachovia). The magnitude of the problem will mean trillions of dollars of losses that need to be absorbed, and businesses may take many years to recover.

- Housing market collapse: U.S. home prices have now fallen by 19.5% from their peak in July 2006[1] and may yet have a long way to go. Prices in Santa Barbara dropped 46% in 2007. Since most Americans have the majority of their net worth in their homes, a large drop in property prices will have a very large negative wealth effect, and consumption will be reduced further.

- Retiring boomers: The U.S. is in the same demographic cycle that Japan was in 1987. It's been twenty years and the Japanese economy is still flat, with real estate values still 70% below their peak in 1989. The massive retirement of the baby boomers could have a strong slowing effect on the U.S. economy for more than ten years.

- Peak Oil: Economic growth and energy consumption are

---

1. S&P Case-Schiller National Home Price Index, Sept. 30, 2008.

directly related. The faster a country's GDP grows, the faster the growth in oil/energy use. Oil production hit a plateau in 2005. If production declines, which many scientists predict, the global GDP will likely decline as well.

• Massive debt: The massive consumer, government, and business debts have to be paid. Either debtors pay their bills, or they default and those owed the money end up losing their loan. Either way, the debt binge will need to be paid off, and that will be a major drag on the economy.

Arguments Against a Long Recession

• Immigration: The United States is one of the few Western countries that have a very positive annual influx of immigrants. Each immigrant adds about $30,000 in economic activity to the country. Continued strong immigration into the U.S. will soften the impact of the retiring boomers.

• Delayed retirement: Boomers will not have the same retirement schedule as the preceding generation. They will likely stay on longer, become self-employed or employed part-time, and will continue to contribute economically to the system.

• Alternative energy: Technology advancements in solar, nuclear, and biofuels will offset the depletion of fossil fuels, thus making Peak Oil a nonevent. Additionally, massive investment in this sector will drive a new equity boom as the world invests capital and hires engineers to replace fossil fuels.

• Interest rate cuts: The Federal Reserve's aggressive reduction in interest rates will stabilize the housing market and banking system.

- Massive government action: The U.S. Treasury, Congress, and Federal Reserve have committed trillions to revive the economy and bolster the markets.

- Jobs: As the boomers retire, there will be a huge demand for employees to replace them, creating a job boom for Gen X, echo boomers (children of the baby boomers), and immigrants, thus driving economic growth.

- Government: The government will cut taxes and increase spending on infrastructure projects. The tax cuts will stimulate economic activity and the government investment will create more employment.

Consequences of a Prolonged Recession

If we enter a deep, prolonged recession, there will be many adverse effects. Psychologically, long economic downturns dampen optimism and hope. Again, an excellent comparison and study is that of Japan over the last two decades. Unemployment will grow as businesses adjust to the slower consumer cycle, and many businesses and people will go bankrupt. In the same way that low unemployment and strong business investment drive economic activity up, higher unemployment and reduced business investment drive the economy down.

Due to human nature, when markets move up, they tend to move up beyond the point of reasonable valuation. And when they go down, like a pendulum, they overshoot to below reasonable valuation. Many investors have profited handsomely by taking advantage of this tendency. Recent examples to the upside are the meteoric dot-com rise in 2000 and the housing boom into 2006. In both cases, the prices of the assets were drastically overpriced in comparison to their long-term trends. Amazon.com hit a high of $113 per share in December 1999. To be fairly valued at that time, Amazon would have had to grow as big as Wal-Mart in ten years—probably a bit optimistic. Over the next two years, Amazon crashed down to a low of $5.51 per share in October 2001—probably a bit pessimistic. By October 2002, Amazon stock climbed to $59.69 per share, and those who invested in Amazon just one year prior made 1000% profit.

I suspect that the housing correction will follow the same pattern over the next several years. When everyone is screaming at the top of their lungs that housing is the worst investment ever and will never recover, then you know that the bottom has occurred. No one knows for sure when that opportune time will occur but even Alan Greenspan said that home prices "are nowhere near the bottom" (CNBC interview, July 31, 2008).

It's likely that politicians will vote to increase taxes and make "the rich" (read: everyone with a middle-class job) pay for the pain and suffering of the poor. For example, Speaker of the House Nancy Pelosi is pushing a $150 billion "stimulus" package to be paid for by the American taxpayer. High taxes do not stimulate growth, but instead just transfer wealth from one class to another, so this will actually have a detrimental effect on stimulating the economy.

The U.S. government's "bailout" will push trillions of dollars into the monetary system, exploding inflation and increasing the cost of living through at least 2010. The likely effects of a global recession on inflation are unclear and could produce two different results: In the near term, the Federal Reserve has decided to try to inflate out of the problem by lowering interest rates and creating lots of money. This action weakens the dollar, thus making everything more expensive. Combined with the tremendous growth of China and India and their demand for all kinds of commodities, price inflation should continue unabated. But if the U.S. and the world experience a strong recession, that could reduce global demand and thus collapse the current boom in commodities. The U.S. Federal Reserve might later decide to combat inflation and jack up interest rates, which could also stop the boom. There are many well-founded arguments for either scenario.

In my opinion, we are in for a long-term, deep recession. People in the U.S. will have to adjust their lifestyles downward, learn to save, and pay off their debt. Daily life will become more expensive, and for those who are already living on the edge of their finances, life could become very difficult. There will still be many great economic opportunities (please read Chapters 14 and 15, "Second Income Opportunities" and "Where We Stuffed Our Money"), but overall, we will need to hunker down and go through a very cold winter cycle before spring emerges.

Scenario Three: The $hit Hits the Fan. The Greater Depression

This is a worst-case scenario. I'm generally an eternal optimist and until recently did not believe that we would have a repeat of the Great Depression. However, with the recent financial nuclear bombs going off around the world in September 2008, I am afraid to say that now I believe this is a much bigger possibility—not definite but very possible. It is prudent to be aware of the possibilities and position yourself and your family accordingly. If I were to give odds on these three scenarios happening, scenario one is 10%, scenario two is 60%, and scenario three is 30%.

Every eighty or so years, the human cycle goes through

a big upheaval called the Kondratieff wave cycle. If you subtract eighty years from 2008, that puts us at 1928, one year
before the beginning of the Great Depression. William Strauss
and Neil Howe's superb book *The Fourth Turning* studies the
eighty-year generational cycle going back five thousand years.
According to their research, in 2000 we entered the twenty-
year winter phase of the generational cycle.

If you just read the headlines from *The New York Times*
or *The Wall Street Journal*, you'll see that there are an inordi-
nate amount of problems around the world: war in Iraq and
Afghanistan; food shortages and riots; inflation; gold, oil,
wheat, and gasoline at record highs; the U.S. dollar setting
new lows; and Paris Hilton making porno films. If you dwell
on this stuff long enough, it can put you in a serious state
of depression. My attitude is, life has always been a roller
coaster, and those who prepare for the dips enjoy the peaks
all the more.

I believe that a lot can be learned from studying system
crashes and learning how people survived and even thrived
during them. One key point to note is that during the Great
Depression, there were more than ten thousand self-made millionaires, more than during the Roaring Twenties preceding
it. All great change brings even greater opportunity for those
who are prepared and willing to act.

Consequences of a Greater Depression

Now for the ugly part. It's worthwhile for you to study the
Great Depression and other economic collapses to help form
your own opinion regarding the likelihood of this scenario
occurring again and the potential problems we might face as a
society. For the sake of argument, let's assume that we have a
Greater Depression fueled by economic collapse, bankruptcies,

high unemployment, Peak Oil, food shortages, and continued war. All the happy stuff!

How will that affect our daily lives? The fear of change is often worse than the change itself. During the Great Depression, from the peak in 1929 to the bottom in 1933, the U.S. GDP contracted 29.7% and unemployment grew to almost 30%. Looked at the other way, 70% of the population still had a job. The 30% drop in GDP was largely a blow-off from the excesses of the speculative credit binge during the 1920s. People still bought food, traveled, fueled their cars, bought and sold homes, sent their kids to school, and so forth. Sure, some people suffered immensely, but many prospered as well. The key is to prepare your mind-set for the possibility of a financial depression and have an action plan (provided in this book) so that you're not caught like a deer in headlights if/when it happens.

Here is a laundry list of things that could happen if the U.S. enters a Greater Depression. These are *possibilities*, not probabilities:

Higher unemployment or underemployment
Wage stagnation or deflation
Devaluation of the dollar that makes travel abroad and imported goods cost-prohibitive
Increased taxes to pay the ever-increasing deficits
Increase in personal bankruptcies
Increase in corporate bankruptcies
Stock market decline of up to 80%
Real estate decline of up to 80% in some areas, leading to massive foreclosures
Expansion of the U.S. war effort to increase our leverage in countries that have critical natural resources
Oil and food shortages
Corporate and government bond defaults

Many banks bankrupt
Government-sponsored enterprises go bankrupt or are
    renationalized[2]
Global famine

It's not a cheerful prospect, but it's important to be aware of the possibilities. That way, if some of them do happen, you won't panic.

A Greater Depression could also have some positive benefits for our society. Consumerism has gone to extreme levels in the U.S. There is ten times the retail space per capita here than in Europe. Americans are infatuated with *stuff*. A depression could shift our culture back toward community and family versus worrying about how big the neighbor's new HDTV is or what chrome package to buy for the Hummer. During troubling times, people realize what's important to them, and it's seldom the fancy car parked in the garage.

---

2. When Freddie Mac and Fannie Mac were taken over by the U.S. government, the entire financial underpinning of the U.S. residential lending market was thrown into turmoil. Other GSEs such as Farmer Mae and Sallie Mae (a former GSE that provides student loans) could also become insolvent.

4

Do I Have Junk in My Trunk?

A Financial Self-Assessment

Everything should be made as simple as possible,
just not one bit simpler.

—Albert Einstein

It always surprises me how little most people know about their own finances. Not until they get into serious financial trouble do they actually assess their situation. It seems that no matter how much money people earn, their expenditures still outpace their income. Maybe it's just a part of human nature.

To best prepare for one of the three possible scenarios discussed in the previous chapter, you need to take a snapshot of your current position so that you know where you might be vulnerable. Until you have a candid—and possibly brutal—assessment of your cash flow and accessible net worth, it will be hard to make correct decisions about your action plan.

PERSONAL SAVINGS RATE
(PERCENT OF DISPOSABLE PERSONAL INCOME)

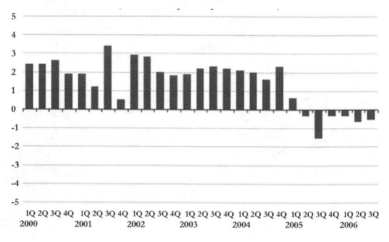

Source: U.S. Bureau of Economic Analysis

There are two basic components of your home's finances that you need to evaluate: your monthly cash flow (income versus expenses) and your real household balance sheet (accessible net worth). I strongly recommend you take thirty minutes or so to go through this exercise. For those of you who run your budget on a software program like Quicken, you can just print out an income statement and balance sheet and see where you are. However, for accessible net worth, there will be some changes you'll need to make.

Your monthly cash flow is just your monthly income minus your monthly expenses. For many Americans, this is a negative number. The aggregate savings rate for the last few years has been below zero (see graph above). This means that most Americans have been and still are spending more than they're making. How have they made up for the shortfall? Up until

2007, many did it by refinancing their homes and replacing the equity with debt. Now that it's much more difficult to get a mortgage, credit card debt is replacing mortgage debt as the new funding source. Not good.

YOUR MONTHLY CASH FLOW

If you don't track all your finances in a personal financial software program, grab a piece of paper and a calculator; or, if you're computer savvy, open up a spreadsheet. Create a section called Income and another one called Expenses. Get your bank statements, credit card bills, pay stubs, etc. for the last couple of months. Use the Monthly Cash Flow Worksheet on page 57 as a guide.

1. Begin by writing down all of your monthly income items. If you have quarterly dividend income or annual income that's consistent, divide that amount by the number of months in the period and use that for your monthly amount. For this exercise, do *not* be optimistic. For example, if you or your spouse are paid on commission, average the monthly commissions on the low end because in an economic downturn, they will likely be lower.

2. Total all of the above and call it your Average Gross Monthly Income.

3. Now we need to evaluate your monthly expenses. If you don't know what all your expenses are because you use a lot of cash, then I highly recommend that you put yourself through the expense-tracking torture program in the next chapter, Escaping Debt Slavery. For the purpose of this exercise, you can make a lump category called ATM Cash Withdrawals and another for your monthly credit card bill.

Just take the last six-month average of each and use that amount.

4. Total all of the above and call it your Total Monthly Cash Flow Expense.

5. Subtract the total expense from your total income, and this tells you what your monthly cash flow is. If it's positive, great job—you're one of the few in the U.S. with positive cash flow, but you're not out of the woods yet. If it's negative, then it's time to take out a meat cleaver and cut into the expense column. Don't feel bad, you're not alone. But now you have the opportunity to take corrective action and fix the problem.

MONTHLY CASH FLOW WORKSHEET

MONTHLY INCOME	MONTHLY EXPENSES/SAVINGS	
Gross salary	Income tax	_____
(before taxes) _____	Medical Insurance	_____
Gross commissions _____	IRA/401(k)	_____
Rental income _____	First mortgage	_____
Dividends _____	Second mortgage	_____
Interest _____	Rent	_____
Investment income _____	Savings	_____
Parental support	Property tax	_____
(money from parents) _____	Mortgage insurance	_____
Child support/alimony _____	Property insurance	_____
	Credit card payment	_____
TOTAL INCOME _____	Credit card interest	_____
	Student loan payment	_____
	Tuition	_____
	Home equity line	
	payment	_____
	Personal credit line	
	payment	_____
	Car payment	_____
	Car insurance	_____
	Groceries	_____
	Utilities	_____
	Entertainment	_____
	Meals out	_____
	Personal	_____
	Clothes	_____
	Medical bills	_____
	Club dues/fees	_____
	Day care	_____
	Business expense	_____
	Gas	_____
	Car repair	_____
	Church/charity	_____
	Vacation	_____
	Recreation	_____
	Other	_____
	TOTAL EXPENSE	_____

TOTAL INCOME – TOTAL EXPENSE = MONTLHY CASH FLOW

_____ – _____ = _____

Your Net Worth

Now we need to take a candid assessment of your household net worth (please see the Personal Net Worth Worksheet below). For this exercise, we will value your assets twice. The first number is what you think they're worth, and the second is what they're worth if you have to sell them quickly. Most people are overly optimistic about the valuation of their assets and possessions. That plasma screen you dropped $5,000 on is not worth $5,000—more like $1,000 or less if you had to sell it fast to raise cash. This exercise will be an eye-opener for some because it will show you how vulnerable you are in an economic downturn.

1. To start, we need to measure all of your assets. Again, make two columns, one for estimated value and the other for liquidation value. Liquidation value is the amount you can sell the item for in thirty days. Surf eBay and craigslist for comparable valuations on household items and cars. For quick sale of your home, check out www.zillow.com for comparable sales in your area. I would then lop 20% off that number since Zillow tends to be a bit optimistic on prices, compared to fast-liquidation value.

2. Add up the values for each column—both estimated and liquidation values.

3. The same exercise will need to be done for liabilities. You only need one column for the actual amount owed.

4. Add up each item in the Liabilities column, and this is what you owe.

5. Subtract your liabilities from your estimated total assets and then also from your liquidation value of assets. The first value is your estimated net worth. The second is your liquid net worth—what you can raise in cash immediately through selling assets.

PERSONAL NET WORTH WORKSHEET

ASSETS			LIABILITIES	
	ESTIMATED VALUE	LIQUIDATION VALUE		
Primary residence	_____	_____	First mortgage	_____
Rental properties	_____	_____	Second mortgage	_____
Vacation home	_____	_____	Home equity line	_____
Other real estate	_____	_____	Other real estate debt	_____
Automobiles (if you lease, this is zero)	_____	_____	Credit card debt	_____
Household goods	_____	_____	Personal credit lines	_____
Jewelry	_____	_____	Business debt	_____
Checking account	_____	_____	Car loans	_____
Savings account	_____	_____	Boat/motorcycle loans	_____
401(k)/IRA	_____	_____	Student loans	_____
Liquid investments (stocks, bonds, CD's, etc)	_____	_____	Consumer loans (jewelry, furniture, etc.)	_____
Illiquid investments (nonpublic company investments or loans, privatepla cements, or loans to friends or family)	_____	_____	IRS debt	_____
			Personal loans from friends or family	_____
Collectibles	_____	_____	Other	_____
Other	_____	_____	TOTAL LIABILITIES	_____
TOTAL ASSETS ESTIMATE VALUE	_____			
TOTAL ASSETS LIQUIDATION VALUE		_____		

ESTIMATED NET WORTH =
TOTAL ASSETS ESTIMATED VALUE – TOTAL LIABILITIES
LIQUID NET WORTH =
TOTAL ASSETS LIQUIDATION VALUE – TOTAL LIABILITIES

If both are positive, congratulations! If both are negative, you have some work to do to get yourself prepared for the upcoming financial storm. If your monthly cash flow is negative and your net worth is negative, you need to act now. Otherwise, life could become very, very challenging in the near future. In Chapter 5, we will go through a detailed debt analysis discussion and ways to get out of debt. Chapter 9 will discuss multiple ways to trim your monthly budget and lower costs.

How Am I Doing?

Let's see how the rest of the country is doing. Here are some net worth statistics for the U.S.

Age: 20–29
Median net worth: $7,900
Top 25%: $36,000
Top 10%: $119,300

Age: 30–39
Median net worth: $44,200
Top 25%: $128,100
Top 10%: $317,800

Age: 40–49
Median net worth: $117,800
Top 25%: $338,100
Top 10%: $719,800

Age: 50–59
Median net worth: $182,300
Top 25%: $563,800
Top 10%: $1,187,600

Age: 60–69
Median net worth: $209,200
Top 25%: $647,200
Top 10%: $1,429,500

Source: Federal Reserve Board's 2004 Survey of Consumer Finances

The Millionaire Next Door: The Surprising Secrets of America's Wealthy (1996) is an excellent book on net worth in the United States and the habits of the frugal, quiet rich. Authors Thomas Stanley and William Danko suggest using a simple formula to determine how much your net worth should be, at any given time in your life. Take your annual pretax income, multiply it by your age, and divide by 10. The result will give you a good standard to judge whether you are on track for a comfortable retirement, and whether you are living above or below your means.

If Jane McFrugal is 40 years old with $100,000 income, her net worth today should be

$$40 \times 100,000 \div 10 = \$400,000$$

If Jane's actual net worth is $800,000, she likely lives a lifestyle well beneath her means, because her actual net worth is double what it needs to be at her age.

Another great tool, the CNN Money website at http://cgi.money.cnn.com/tools/networth_ageincome/index.html, asks your age and income and tells you what your peer group median net worth is by age group and income. These are good guides and reference points but by no means absolute. A major factor that these tools do not consider is where you live. A person who lives in Manhattan, an extremely high-cost area, needs a much higher net worth than a person who lives in Birmingham, Alabama. The cost of living in Manhattan is two to three times that of other places in the United States, so in times of financial duress, you can burn through your net worth rather quickly there.

FURTHER ASSET ANALYSIS

The real estate market in many areas of the United States is currently in free fall. Most Americans have the largest percentage of their net worth tied up in their primary residence, so the deflation of home prices is rather painful. Many who purchased a home after 2004 are now sitting on a mortgage larger than the value of their home. Because of the rapid increase in home prices since 2001, the monthly payment on a thirty-year fixed loan in most areas is substantially higher than the monthly rent for the same home. We sold our home in the fall of 2006 and have been renting since. Our monthly rent of $2,500 is half what the monthly mortgage payment with taxes and insurance is. Since prices are now going down in the Seattle area, we're saving $2,500 per month in mortgage payments and property taxes, repair costs, and the 10% price deflation that has occurred so far. A detailed housing analysis given in Chapter 6, "Real Estate: Is It a Home or a Prison?" on debt analysis will help you to reduce costs and improving cash flow.

I strongly recommend that you analyze your local real estate market and your current situation in detail. If you purchased your home ten or more years ago with a normal fifteen- or thirty-year fixed mortgage and haven't succumbed to the refinance or home equity loan temptation, then you're probably in fine shape. If you own vacation properties or rentals, also do analyses for those respective markets.

Look in detail at your stock and bond portfolio and analyze it for safety and volatility. Many investors received an unpleasant surprise in the fall of 2007 when they invested in a money market fund that they thought was perfectly safe, to discover later that the fund was heavily invested in mortgage-backed securities and lost 80% of its value. As Will Rogers famously pointed out, return *of* capital is more important than return *on* capital. Skip to the last chapter to see where we stuffed our money for safety and profitability.

5

Escaping Debt Slavery

Taking Back Your Freedom

Some debts are fun when you are acquiring them, but none are fun when you set about retiring them.
Ogden Nash

I owe, I owe. So off to work I go.
—Bumper sticker

ebt is truly the scourge of mankind. We enter into it willingly, looking at it as free money and not realizing the cost of paying it back. Debt is not something to be taken lightly. The serious side to debt is that it forces a fear-based mentality on those who have it. How can you be free to create a great life for yourself if someone or some institution is in control of your life? Living in constant fear of obligations beyond your capacity to pay, or living on income that is not really yours, is crippling.

I eschew debt largely because I was raised by my mother, who set an excellent example that you can achieve your dreams and goals in life without racking up debt. Back then, divorced women had a hard time getting mortgages and credit cards, which turned out to be a blessing in disguise for us. My mother was required to draw upon her own resourcefulness, talent, and wit for us to survive financially. By the way, she also put herself through law school without accumulating student debt, and owned a home with no mortgage. Her example set in my mind an important philosophy about money: You pay for what you can. And if you don't have the money, you save up for it.

Many of us slip into debt without even being aware of it. We live in a culture of excuses and a mind-set that money is hard to come by. Debt is the easy solution. But debt is a solution with a heavy price to pay: the loss of control. The minute we take on debt, we place the control of our lives in the hands of someone or something else.

Getting out of this mentality will require a shift in thinking. Accept that you can still have what you want in life without accumulating debt. There are lots of ways to get what you want. Debt does not have to be the vehicle, nor does it need to have a place in your life.

The number one goal of those living with debt should be to get out of debt. If you have debt, make a promise to yourself to pay it off as soon as you can. And while you're paying it off, do not take on even one cent more in debt. Set a time frame for yourself, pick a date in the future, and make a big sign that reads, "I Will Be Debt Free by x Date," and put it in a prominent location where you can see it every day—perhaps on your refrigerator or bathroom mirror.

Pretty Little Debt Machine

The American lifestyle has largely been funded by debt, rather than by creating anything of value. If you give a person $100,000 in credit cards, they can live pretty nicely for a year or two, but once that credit runs out, the pain begins. America as a whole has been accumulating massive debts that have funded the opulent lifestyle of the last two decades. The pundits like to call it the miracle of modern finance, but in reality it's just borrowing from the future to pay for today.

The following graph clearly shows that we have used debt rather than equity to fund ourselves. Since 1964, adjusted for inflation, average household income has grown annually by 4.5%. Household income has grown not because individual wages have gone up, but because women began entering the workforce in large numbers. Inflation-adjusted wages since 1972 have actually gone down by 1%! During the same period, inflation-adjusted household debt has grown annually by 7.6%. This is completely unsustainable and will lead to tremendous problems. The bottom line is that you have to get out of debt as soon as possible and stop taking on new debt.

U.S. INCOMES VERSUS DEBT, PERCENTAGE GROWTH

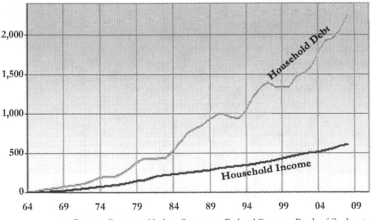

Source: Bureau of Labor Statistics, Federal Reserve Bank of St. Louis

CREDIT CARDS

According to www.cardweb.com, the average U.S. credit card debt is $8,000 per family. As usual, statistics are manipulated greatly to make sensational news. Here are some actual stats from the Federal Reserve 2001 analysis of credit card debt:

- 23.8% of American households have no credit cards at all.
- 31.2% of American households paid off their most recent credit card bills in full.
- 55% of households carry no credit card debt.
- Only 4% owe more than $10,500, and 1% more than $21,400, notes MSN Money writer Liz Pulliam Weston.

The households in the 55% category are called deadbeats by the credit card industry because they do not generate much revenue. The industry's ideal clients are those who spend uncontrollably and are buried in debt. I see the credit card business as similar to the loan shark and payday loan companies. For those of us who pay off our cards every month or carry them just for emergencies, credit cards are a convenient way to purchase things. But many look at their credit cards as money, not debt, and spend away. Credit card companies have really mastered how to milk as much money from the consumer as they can. On its website, Consumers' Defense (www.consumersdefense.com) points out that the CEO of Providian Financial Corporate (a major credit card company) stated it best: "The goal is to squeeze out enough revenue and get customers to sit still for the squeeze."

It's easy to get dinged by dirty tricks of the credit card companies. Here is a list of some of the payment tactics they hide from the cardholder, according to Consumers' Defense:

Changing payment deadlines
Changing credit limits

Charging for unneeded services like credit insurance
Illegally high interest rates
Illegal late fees
Over-the-limit fees
Draconian collection tactics such as relentless phone calls and
    threats of legal action
Changing the terms of the credit card agreement without noti-
    fication or the card member's consent

If you can decipher the overly verbose legalese in your
credit card agreement, you'll find that credit card companies
can increase your interest rates if you're late for a payment on a
different credit card. These guys are like sharks that smell blood
in the water, and if they see you struggle to make a payment,
they will jack up your rates. They have algorithms that classify
you based on your credit score, debt balance, and payment history to maximize what rates they can charge you.

Do not carry credit card debt, and if you have it, get out
of it by paying more than the minimum payment each month.
The minimum payment keeps you forever in debt slavery. Cut
your expenses and pay these off as fast as you can. You're being
charged between 10% and 29.9% annually for this money,
which is far higher than the returns you're likely getting on
your investments. Pay off the credit card debt and shred the
cards if you have a hard time controlling yourself.

Here are six steps for getting rid of credit card debt:

1. Cut up your cards and stop using them.

2. Call 1-888-5-OptOut (888-567-8688) to stop receiving
   new credit card offers. This will help you avoid the temp-
   tations they present.

3. Establish a budget to pay far more than the monthly minimum.

4. Pay off the cards with the highest interest rates first and work your way down.

5. Reduce your annual interest rate. Call the credit card company and threaten to switch if you don't get a lower rate. You can often knock the rate down from 20% to as low as 11% or 12%. Always seek out the best possible interest rates, even if that means transferring balances to a zero- or low-interest card periodically.

6. Consolidate your debt. See if you can transfer the amount owed on the highest cards to those with lower interest. The current upheaval in the credit markets might make this difficult, but try anyway.

Credit card debt can also be discharged through bankruptcy, but recent government laws have made it easier for credit card companies to file nondischargeable claims against card holders. To qualify for this claim, the card companies have to prove either that the application for the card was fraudulent or more commonly, that the card holder had no intention of paying down the account.

If you plan to file bankruptcy (not recommended unless you have absolutely no choice), the following actions should be taken to help reduce the chances of a nondischargeable claim being filed against you:

Avoid using credit cards 60 days before filing
Avoid using a newly issued card
Avoid any cash advances
Avoid using one card to pay for another
Do not exceed your credit limit
Avoid using the card when unemployed or without the ability to pay the debt back

Avoid having a large balance at filing

Avoid using the card after consulting an attorney

Leases (Cars, Boats, Etc.)

Leasing generally doesn't make financial sense unless you own your own business and can deduct the lease payments for tax purposes. I know, I know, they like to say that if you can drive it, fly it, or float it, you should lease it. I adamantly disagree. It's far more financially savvy to buy a car that's a couple years old, after the most substantial depreciation has already occurred. Read the section on car purchases in How to Get Stuff Cheap to learn how you can basically drive for free.

If you have a lease, what can you do? Most leasing contracts allow you to get out of your lease if you can find a creditworthy person to take it over. A great website that brokers these transactions is www.leasetrader.com. It features an online catalogue of leased vehicles looking for new owners. The only caveat is that most banks will allow you to do this only once, so if you acquired the leased vehicle from someone else, you will likely not be allowed to trade out the vehicle. Another option is that if you lease the vehicle from a dealership, you can often negotiate a trade-in for a used one. You will need to sharpen your negotiating skills, however, since the dealer will be in the power position. Of course, pleading poverty and probability of default might get them to move in your direction. A few tears never hurt either, especially since most car salesmen are men, and like most men, they are clueless when the waterworks begin to flow.

Student Debt

Student loans are now the number one source of funds for tuition. Recently, with the spread of the credit crisis, students are finding it much more difficult to qualify for those loans. In concept, they are a great idea because they help students to acquire college degrees. However, they also saddle students with substantial debt before they even enter the workforce. It's better for students to have a part-time job and take longer to get their education than for them to take on large amounts of debt. An additional benefit of working for your education is that you appreciate it far more than you would if it were paid for with loans or parental welfare. And the best-case scenario is getting your education for free by choosing the right major.[1]

If you fail to make payments on your student loan, then the government can garnish your wages for payment. There have even been cases where the parents have been held financially responsible for their child's failure to make the loan payments. Changes in the Bankruptcy Code in 1998 now make student loan debt nondischargeable, regardless of the amount or age of the loan. The only way borrowers can get the loan discharged is if he or she can prove that payment of the loan will create an undue hardship on the borrower or the borrower's family. Basically, payment of the loan will need to put the borrower below the poverty line before it can be discharged. The good news is that lenders are able to garnish only up to 10% of your take-home pay to pay for student loans, so the burden is not too onerous.

---

1. For women, majoring in math, science, or engineering is the quickest, dirtiest way to get a free education. There are loads of grants for women who choose the road less traveled and major in any of these tough subjects. Why go to into student debt when you can get your master's and Ph.D. for free? Additionally, these degrees set you up for a cushy job in academia as a researcher or professor. Professors are paid nicely, have tons of time off, and enjoy a great lifestyle. It's a happy career choice.

The key strategy for managing student loans is to be realistic about what your after-graduation income will be and what your payments are. It's better to take six or more years to get a degree while working part-time than to put yourself in heavy debt to finish "on time."

IRS DEBT

The IRS is the last collection agency you want on your back. They make the Mafia look like Boy Scouts. If the IRS is after you, the deck is stacked against you from the get-go. The IRS even has its own tax courts if you have to go to trial. The agency is able to garnish your wages, take your house, lien your bank accounts, and all sorts of other wonderful things.

That's the bad news. The good news is that if you take a nonadversarial approach, you can usually negotiate payment plans and the like.

Bankruptcy can, under certain circumstances, discharge an IRS debt. To qualify for debt discharge, the following conditions must be met:

The debt must be from taxable income.
It must be from a tax return that is at least three years old.
Two years must have passed since the tax return was filed.
At least 240 days must have passed since an "Offer in Compromise" has been terminated.

There are other minor factors that the IRS takes into consideration. As always, you should consult professionals if this is your situation. I would not recommend doing this on your own.

CREDIT SCORES

I rather loathe the credit score system and find it extremely demeaning that people are measured by their "creditworthiness." It seems that our importance is based on our ability to consume, rather than our ability to produce. The scary side to the credit score system is that it falsely links financial stability to a high score, misleading many credit card addicts into believing they are financially stable because they have high FICO scores. If you follow much of the advice of this book, you will (eventually) have good credit, but the best part is that you shouldn't need it, since you'll be paying cash for everything.

So, what is a FICO score? FICO stands for Fair Isaac Corporation, the geniuses behind this diabolical system. FICO was developed as a way to distill all credit information down to a simple number that helps lenders determine a borrower's ability to pay. According to myFICO (myfico.com), the score incorporates the following factors:

35% - Payment history
30% - Amounts owed
15% - Length of credit history
10% - Types of credit used
10% - New credit

FICO SCORE BREAKDOWN

FICO 700 AND UP
Considered excellent
Generally rated as A quality
Will generally get the best interest rates and terms
About 60% of the U.S. population

FICO 600–699
Considered good
Generally rated as B quality
Will have access to good rates, but will not qualify for the best
   rates and terms
27% of the population

FICO 500–599
Considered risky credit
Generally rated as C quality
May still qualify for a loan, but will have to pay two percentage
   points more than the A group
12% of the population

FICO 400–499
Considered very risky credit
Generally rated as D quality
May still be eligible or a loan, but will have to pay extremely
   high interest rates
1% of the population

   Scores are important and can substantially affect its terms
if you plan on getting a loan. If your FICO is above 720, you're
in great shape and should qualify for the best prime rates and
terms. According to FICO, 60% of Americans are above 700
and have very good credit. Where the difference shows up is
in the 600s, and one point can make a difference; a person
with a 674 FICO score will pay an interest rate 1% higher
than a person with 675. On a $250,000 mortgage, that is
$200 per month, or $75,000 over the life of a thirty-year loan.
When you get to the low 600s, the difference becomes even
more extreme. A person with a FICO score of 619 will pay
almost double the interest of a person with a 720 score. On

the same $250,000 loan, this equates to $375,000 over the life of the loan.

Regardless of what you think about FICO scores, they are extremely important if you plan on getting a loan. If your score is not good, doing the following will help to improve your credit over time. First, order your credit reports from www.freecreditreport.com or www.annualcreditreport.com. They will provide you with your credit history as recorded by Equifax, Transunion, and Experian. You can usually download the report online or have it mailed to you. Any discrepancies you see in your report should be reported immediately; call the creditors who filed the claim and try to clear up the situation. If a creditor made an error, demand that they retract it. If they are correct, work out a payment plan to make the debt current.

Here are other things you can do to improve your score:

- Pay your bills on time.

- Keep your bills current.

- Collections stay on your credit report for seven years, so avoid them at all costs.

- If you're in trouble, contact your creditors; do not wait for them to contact you.

- Keep your balances on all your revolving credit low. Don't run up large balances that you hold over time.

- Don't have more credit cards than you need. Too much access to credit can actually lower your score.

- Don't open too many credit accounts too quickly. A young average account age is detrimental to your score.

- Do your loan shopping in a set window of time. The credit

agencies track searches on your credit history, so a lot of searches over a drawn-out period of time will adversely impact your credit score.

- If you have had credit problems, you can reestablish your credit history by opening new accounts and paying them on time.

- Checking your own credit report does not affect your score as long as you do it through an authorized agency (see above).

- Get only the credit accounts you need.

- Use your credit responsibly, pay your bills, and you will be able to establish good credit once again.

EXPENSE TRACKING WITH CHINESE WATER TORTURE

Forget waterboarding. Here's a torture program that will get you results. Now we're getting down to the nitty-gritty reality of money—where it goes, and why it keeps flying out of your wallet. Grab a stiff drink and sit down, because what I'm about to say will either make you chuck this book across the room (an expensive proposition, if you're reading it on your computer!) or howl uncontrollably. Here it is: If you want to get control of your money and your spending, you need to track every single penny you spend for an entire month. This grueling and arduous process will leave you with the realities of exactly where your money goes every month.

"Incidentals" can do us in one magazine at a time. You know what I mean—a bottled water here, a Big Mac there, and before you know it, you're blowing a grand a month on mocha lattes and other incidentals. Now, before you say you "know" what this all adds up to for yourself, let me interrupt.

I guarantee that you don't. It's not enough to guess. Write down all of your purchases, big and small, down to the last postage stamp. Keep a little notebook and pen with you at all times. If you want to get fancy, you can take the data and put it through Quicken, or some other financial software, and run scary charts and graphs displaying the monetary consequences of your Starbucks low-fat blueberry muffin addiction. You'll be amazed, horrified, and shocked at how much money you're pissing away on nothing of value.

The beauty of this process is twofold. First, you'll come to detest spending, because it will involve having to whip out your little notebook and document the expense. And you'll probably carry a little of this loathing for spending with you for the rest of your life. Luckily for you, that means dollars in the bank over the long term. The second benefit is that suddenly you'll be able to pinpoint where you're bleeding money so you can stop it. Knowing is half the battle, so do it.

Recession Heat Index			
	Smokin' Hot	**Tepid**	**Chilled**
Concerns	Keeping a roof over your head	Keeping your sanity	Keeping up with the Joneses
Wardrobe Financing	Cash	Credit cards	Home equity line of credit (HELOC)
Tuition source	Mowing lawns	Mom and Dad	Student loans

6

Real Estate: Is It a Home or a Prison?

Dump It, Hold It, or Borrow?

Credit buying is much like being drunk. The buzz happens immediately and gives you a lift. . . . The hangover comes the day after.
—Joyce Brothers

Back in 2006, when the real estate market in Seattle was on fire, my husband and I made a bold move. We sold our house at the end of the year, took our capital gains, moved our family out, and shacked up in a rental. Yes, a rental. In our culture, which touts home ownership as the key to a fabulous marriage, a stable life, and great hair even when it's raining, the word *renting* sounds downright dirty. Even I thought at first that renting seemed a little seedy. What would the neighbors think? Fortunately, the opposite was true. We have a fantastic relationship with our neighbors in our rental neighborhood. We plant flowers and don't let our children throw darts at the walls. We care for our rental property just as the owner would, if not better. The only difference is that someone else holds the debt on the house in which we reside.

After the real estate market in Seattle started tanking, I realized that selling our house and renting was one of the smartest financial decisions we've ever made. We have no debt, no car payments, and no mortgage. We lie awake at night worrying about nothing. It's a tremendous feeling of freedom.

Not that I'm not saying you shouldn't buy or own a home. But I am saying that you need to look at a multitude of factors when making the decision whether to buy or rent. For the last decade, the public was bombarded daily with the message that everyone in the U.S. should own a home. It became almost an entitlement mentality, and almost anyone could get a mortgage. Many people would buy a home even if they knew they were going to move in two years. During the bubble days, this worked out okay, but now we're moving into a whole new market cycle.

Here are some questions to consider when you make the decision to buy or rent:

For how long do you plan to live in this home?
What is the rent versus mortgage payment ratio?
What is the expected annual appreciation? (Be conservative.)
What are the property taxes?
What are the insurance and maintenance costs?

Yahoo has an excellent rent-versus-own calculator: http://realestate.yahoo.com/calculators/rent_vs_own.html.
As an example, I put the home Dan and I are currently rent-

ing into the Yahoo calculator to examine cost to rent versus cost to buy. We pay $2,500 for rent, and the home is valued at $650,000. I assumed a thirty-year mortgage at 6.5% on $480,000, with a down payment of 20%, and that we plan to stay in the home for ten years. This mortgage rate is probably a bit low, since we would require a jumbo mortgage, and those rates are 7% or higher right now. I also assumed annual appreciation of just 2%, which is actually very generous because the real estate bubble will likely deflate for many years. Though 2% is below the historical average of 3%, homes should track below the historical average over the next ten years. Here are the results.

Analysis	Rent	Buy
Rent and fees	392,430	
Mortgage payments		367,572
Property insurance		21,899
Property taxes		59,128
Maintenance		40,000
Opportunity cost[1]		148,026
Tax savings		(86,645)
Appreciation[2]		(143,780)
Total cost	**392,430**	**406,201**
Present value at inflation	321,888	335,795
Difference		**(13,907)**

1. Opportunity cost is the interest you would make on the down payment. In this example, we assumed we would make an 8% taxable return on the $170,000 we would have spent on the down payment, compounded over ten years. After taxes, this equals $148,026.
2. Appreciation is the increasing value of the home over time.

Based on these assumptions, we will save almost $14,000 by renting versus buying over ten years. If we were to stay in the home just five years, we would save more than $18,000, assuming that the house actually goes up in price. I believe it will actually reprice down to about $500,000 over the next five years, in which case we'll actually save $168,000!

The bottom line is that it's smart to rent if:

• You don't plan on being in the home for more than five years. The cost of selling your home is close to 10% when you factor in taxes, Realtor fees, and moving expenses.

• You don't think the home is going to appreciate over the period you'll be living in it.

• The ratio of home value to annual rent in your area is low or normal. In the Seattle area, it is 22 to 1 (so a $500,000 house is about $1,900 per month to rent). The normal ratio of home value to annual rent should be 12 to 1. In some cities, it is 30 to 1, placing a huge cost premium on ownership.

It's smart to buy a home if:

• The home value to annual rent ratio is in a normal range.

• You plan to live in the home for more than five years.

• You believe that home values will at least stay flat, if not increase.

Beware the National Association of Realtors' (NAR) propaganda machine. According to NAR's latest marketing campaign, to which I am subjected daily on the radio, "On average, home prices almost double every ten years. Now is a great time to buy a house and begin your path to long-term wealth." If you read the fine print, you will find that this study was based on the last thirty years of market data and includes one of the largest real estate bubbles in U.S. history. I prefer looking at a longer-term perspective that takes into account the major economic ups and downs and not just the boom times. One study, by Yale finance and economics professor Robert J. Shiller, author of *Irrational Exuberance*, argues that residential real estate returns are far worse than claimed. His study dates back to 1890, and he contends that only twice has real estate outperformed the general markets: right after World War II and during the latest bubble, from 1998 to 2005. Historical housing returns average about 3% a year, barely above the inflation rate. (I would argue that it is *below* the inflation rate, based on the way inflation is calculated.) Professor Shiller states further that if the U.S. reverts to the mean of 3%, we could face many years of losses.

Here's a more recent example of real estate market corrections. In 1989, one prefecture (a downtown block) of Tokyo was valued higher than the entire country of Canada. Homes purchased in Japan in the late 1980s are, twenty years later, still valued at only 50% of their purchase price. The U.S. is entering the same demographic retirement downturn that Japan entered in 1989. It is very possible that housing prices here will stay depressed for a very, very long time.

Do not look at your home as an investment. Sometimes it's an investment, and a very smart one. Other times it can be a giant liability. As I said earlier, your home is where you live and not a savings account. In fact, in many of the markets right now, the cost of ownership far exceeds the equivalent rental cost for the first ten years if you assume the historical 3% price appreciation. I am definitely not suggesting that you shouldn't buy a home. I just don't think right now is the right time to buy depending on which market you live in. Certain markets have started to bottom, but others, like Seattle, have just started their decline.

Mortgage Debt

The housing market peaked in late 2006, and as of March 2008, it has been in free fall with no bottom in sight. You need to sit down and seriously evaluate your mortgage situation. If you purchased or refinanced your home to take out equity in the last three or four years, there is a good chance you have no equity or even negative equity in your home.

A home is more than just an asset; there is a huge emotional attachment to it. You need to step back and try to be objective. Too many people allow their emotional attachment to things cloud their judgment, and they end up losing everything. CBS News Online summed it up best,[1] pointing out that over the last decade, Americans have supported themselves by sucking money out of their homes, rather than earning money the old fashioned way—by working. This has created an unsustainable false reality. Owning a home should remain a goal, but it creates social good only if buyers are building equity—which is a long-term investment in not only the home but also the community. A home without equity is just a debt-laden rental.

According to an analysis and forecast by demographic economist Harry Dent (www.hsdent.com), during this bubble burst, home values could decline back to where they were in 1999—an average of 50%. In some of the overheated markets like Miami, Las Vegas, and California, the declines could be as severe as 80%. This is a brutal assessment, but it also gives you a good idea of how bad things could get.

---

1. CBS News Online, "Waking Up from the American Dream," May 2, 2008.

To evaluate your own position, you first need to look at your mortgage documents and understand what type of mortgage you have to see if you are sitting on a time bomb. Here is a brief description of the various types:

Prime: This is the highest-quality mortgage loan. The borrower has a credit score of 680 or higher, fully documents income and assets, has a debt-to-income ratio that does not exceed 35%, and puts at least 20% down on the purchase.

Agency: This mortgage is guaranteed by one of the Federal GSEs (government-sponsored enterprises), Fannie Mae or Freddie Mac. Because the loan is secured, interest rates are usually rather low. Neither agency has reported its balance sheet to the GAO (government accounting office) in the last three years. Many analysts suspect that they could be insolvent, even with their recent government backing, which would be disastrous if true.

Alt-A: This is a type of U.S. mortgage that, for various reasons, is considered riskier than "prime" and less risky than "subprime" (the riskiest category). Interest rates, which are determined by credit risk, tend to be between those of prime and subprime home loans. These loans are often low-document/no-document loans (i.e., stated income) that rely mainly on the credit rating of the applicant.

Subprime: This type of mortgage is normally made out to borrowers with lower credit ratings (below 600). A conventional mortgage is not available because the lender views the borrower as having a larger-than-average risk of defaulting on the loan. Interest rates on subprime mortgages are usually much higher than conventional mortgages, and many

were made with teaser introductory rates and low documen-
tation requirements that just asked for trouble . . . and they
got it.

Optional Adjustable Rate: This is an adjustable-rate mortgage
(ARM) that allows the borrower to choose from three types
of payment each month. The borrower can make a standard
mortgage payment (principal, interest, taxes, and insurance,
also known as PITI) that will pay off the loan off in fifteen
or thirty years. Or, the borrower can choose to pay only the
interest charged in the previous month. Finally, the borrower
can make a minimum payment that doesn't even cover the
interest—a convenient option when times are tight, but one
that increases the total amount owed on the mortgage. Most
optional ARMs have absurd introductory interest rates that
are simply teasers, sometimes below 2%. Those rates usually
last a month or two, after which they begin to rise with clock-
work regularity. The truly hidden risk in an optional ARM
is that although the interest rate changes every month, the
required monthly payment changes only once a year, meaning
you might be making significant underpayments that will add
to the cost of your loan. Additionally, if the principal on the
loan grows to a certain amount because of these below-interest
payments, the loan automatically resets to a much higher payment rate. These are a potential nuclear bomb if you're not
careful.

The following graph shows when various mortgages will
reset. As you can see, we are in the middle of the subprime
resets, which is why we're seeing so much press about rising
foreclosures and banking losses. Now, look at the optional
ARMs. Just as the subprime resets are slowing down, the
Optional ARMs start ramping up. If you think the subprime
fiasco is ugly now, just wait.

Monthly Mortgage Rate Resets
(First Reset in Billions of U.S. Dollars)

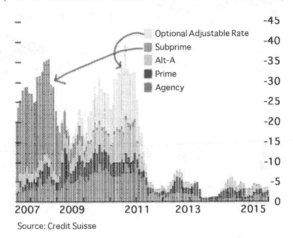

Source: Credit Suisse

Once you have determined the type of mortgage you have, you then need to figure out whether you'll have an interest rate reset, and if so, what that rate likely will be. ARMs are tied to LIBOR[2] and not the Federal Reserve rate. The Fed has been cutting rates aggressively, but that has not shown up in ARM rates because European rates, which help determine LIBOR, have been increasing to combat inflation.

If you currently have a subprime or optional ARM, the clock on the time bomb you call your home is ticking. If you have a lot of equity in the home (probably not the case), then you should begin aggressively shopping for refinancing into a more secure mortgage like an alt-A, agency, or prime, if you

---

2. London Interbank Offered Rate is the interest rate that the international banks charge for lending money. The rate is set more by global interest rates than U.S. interest rates, so rate reductions in the U.S. have little effect on it.

qualify. If you do not qualify and are stuck where you are, then it's time to make some hard decisions.

If you have little or no equity in your home or face a mortgage rate reset that you cannot afford, there are two numbers you should look at immediately. First, what is the rent for a comparable home in your market? Second, what is the ratio of the mortgage to your household income? In many of the coastal (expensive) markets, rents can be half or less of a mortgage (excluding the teaser rates that the lender hooked people in with). If this is the case, why would you want to pay double the monthly rental payment for a house that's depreciating in value? The ratio of a mortgage to household income tells you what you can afford. Historically, the ratio is between 2.5 and 3 to 1. In other words, if your household income is $100,000, you can comfortably afford a home priced from $250,000 to $300,000. Many people were getting mortgages at 10 to 1 or even higher. If you're around 3 to 1 and your income is stable, then you should be able to weather the storm. If your ratio is higher than that, you might consider selling or tightening your expenditures elsewhere.

Let's assume that you're in the mortgage time bomb category or are sitting on a house that's underwater, and you want to get out. What do you do? Worst-case scenario is a bank foreclosure. The good news is that you can live payment free for six months or more while the bank is trying to foreclose on you. Another option is the short sale. This is selling your home for less than you owe on it. Here are some of the ins and outs of both.

Second Mortgages and Home Equity Lines of Credit: Home equity lines of credit (HELOC) and second mortgages are used interchangeably. In the last several years, mortgage brokers would allow a buyer to use a HELOC as the 20% down payment for the purchase instead of a cash deposit. A HELOC usually has an interest rate that adjusts with LIBOR or the U.S. prime rate. It can be paid down and drawn upon.

Depending on the state, if a HELOC is used in the purchase of the home, it can be considered a nonrecourse loan and thus can be backed only by the collateral of the property. (See the next section for lists of recourse and nonrecourse states.) If the HELOC was taken out after the purchase, its recourse status is determined on a case-by-case basis for the state you are in and also by the type of HELOC it is. (Please see the next section, Foreclosure, for more information on recourse versus nonrecourse states.) The tax consequences of a foreclosure or short sale with a HELOC are generally the same as the consequences discussed in the previous chapter. As always, please consult a tax or legal professional about the specific laws of your state and the HELOC agreement. It is better to be prepared than surprised.

Many borrowers use their HELOC to pay off their credit cards. In concept, this is a great idea, because you're replacing high-interest debt with lower-interest debt (since the HELOC is backed by the equity in your home). But in practice, these credit lines are used to pay off credit cards and then those credit cards are run up again. So if you plan to use the HELOC to pay off a credit card account, please cut up your cards to remove all temptation!

Sticking It to the Bank

Foreclosure

First, this is not the end of the world. You are one of many, and the banks are overwhelmed right now. Learn what your rights are and do not let the bank intimidate you. The banker's job is to get you to pay what you owe or get you out of the house so the bank can sell it. Because of the backlog of foreclosures, the process is taking longer than normal, which means longer payment-free living and more time to save up your money for rent for the home you'll move into. Yes, your credit rating will take a hit and it's emotionally painful, but you'll get over it. Life goes on.

There are two types of foreclosure: administrative (nonjudicial)[3] and judicial. Most lenders choose the administrative foreclosure process because it's much faster. The judicial process can take years and a lender won't usually go that route unless the borrower has a high net worth and is worth going after. For most, the nonjudicial process will apply.

When thinking about foreclosure, you should consider whether you live in a recourse or nonrecourse state. If you're in a nonrecourse state, the lender can generally take only your home and not come after your other assets. If you live in a recourse state, the lender can go after all of your assets, not just your home. Most real estate brokers or mortgage brokers in your area can tell you. Here is a list of some nonrecourse states: Alabama, Alaska, Arizona, Arkansas, California (only for nonjudicial foreclosure), Colorado, Washington, D.C., Georgia, Hawaii, Idaho, Mississippi, Missouri, Montana (only for nonjudicial foreclosure), New Hampshire, Oregon, Tennessee, Virginia, Washington (only for nonjudicial foreclosure), and West Virginia.

These states allow for nonjudicial foreclosure but also allow the lender to pursue an additional deficiency judgment against the borrower: Michigan, Minnesota, North Carolina, Rhode

---

3. "Nonjudicial" means an administrative process that doesn't go to trial. The lender just files the documents and the process follows a very defined time line. "Judicial" means the foreclosure has to go to court and usually takes a couple of years to resolve.

Island, South Dakota, Utah, and Wyoming. This means that they can come after your other assets.

Just because you have a mortgage in one of the above states does not necessarily mean that you have a "get out of jail free" card. Please review your loan documents, and we strongly recommend you consult an attorney who specializes in real estate law. There are a lot of laws to protect the consumer, and educating yourself and understanding your rights will help you greatly in deciding a course of action. If you have refinanced or have a second mortgage, they are usually recourse loans, so your options there are more limited but still not insurmountable. Banks are in so much pain right now that those who are in distressful situations (people who have very few assets) have some good negotiating leverage. From the bank's perspective, something is better than nothing.

Here is a wicked little secret the mortgage industry is desperately trying to keep out of the press. In all their frenzied greed, the financial establishments that were packaging up all these disastrous mortgages and selling them off so they could collect fees forgot to do the paperwork. Many of these mortgages have been resold several times. Guess what? The deeds were never properly transferred! What does this mean? Well, Deutsche Bank tried to foreclose on a party in the Midwest. That party requested that it provide proof of ownership, i.e., the title to the property. Deutsche Bank could not. Therefore, it could not prove that it had the right to foreclose. The case went all the way to the regional federal court and the bank lost. Until the title is tracked down and properly transferred, no one owns the home, so the borrower basically gets to live there payment free. If you're being foreclosed upon, demand that the bank that owns your mortgage produce proof that it has title to the property. It's a long shot, but many more of these situations are turning up and you might just get lucky!

Avoiding Foreclosure

After you have assessed your financial situation and have a decent understanding of your mortgage, there are several things you can do to help avoid foreclosure.

Refinance

If you have an ARM that will reset soon, immediately talk with other mortgage lenders to see if you can refinance into a fixed-rate mortgage. Short-term interest rates will continue to climb, so it's smart to lock in a fixed rate now if you can. Currently, fixed rates are at or below the current ARM rates. However, since you're paying down your principal faster with a fixed rate, the monthly payment will likely be higher than your current ARM's rates. In order to refinance, you will have to qualify and have at least 20% equity in your home.

Forbearance

If you're in a short-term financial crunch, you can ask your lender to let you skip a couple of payments. You'll still owe the money and the lender will still charge you interest, but it may allow you some breathing room. The key point is to know your situation and be proactive with your creditors, rather than just skipping a payment without warning them.

Mortgage Relief

If you know that you won't be able to make payments, you can ask the lender to postpone foreclosure. Normally, if you stop payments, your home will be foreclosed upon within 90 to 180 days. You can request a delay from your lender that will allow you to get your finances in order and hopefully save your home from foreclosure.

REQUEST A LOAN MODIFICATION

If you are facing a situation where you even *think* you're going to miss payments, call your lender and see if you can restructure your loan to one that meets your financial requirements. An example would be to ask for an interest-only loan with a five-year term, giving you a chance to get your finances in order and allowing time for the mortgage system to fix itself. I cannot stress this enough—if there's even a chance you won't be able to pay your mortgage, it behooves you greatly to be proactive and approach the bank immediately and with urgency. Now is not the time for pride. You need to make the bank think you are somewhat desperate. Banks certainly do not like holding bad assets, and they do not want to foreclose. The banks have an incentive to work with you on giving you a payment plan you can afford. For them, getting some kind of payment from you is better than getting no payment and having to go through the foreclosure process. Don't be shy. Be responsible and proactive, and ask for exactly what you want. Loan modifications were very popular during the Great Depression as well. Banks were willing to bend and give people interest-only rates for the duration of the Great Depression. Today, banks have almost overnight created and staffed large loan modification departments to handle these requests. They are granting these requests, but you have to ask.

As a side note, don't expect your Realtor or your mortgage broker to understand or support your decision to get a loan modification. They make no money off these transactions, so they are not "pushing" them.

Offer to Leave: Deed in Lieu of Foreclosure

You can talk to the bank and offer to leave the house in great condition, turning the home and the deed over to it voluntarily, without going through the foreclosure process. In exchange, you get to walk away owing nothing to the bank. The advantage to the bank is that it can avoid the $40,000 cost involved in a formal foreclosure process. The advantage to you is that the process is quicker and easier than a foreclosure, saves you from having your name associated with a foreclosure in public records, and should keep the foreclosure off your credit report. If you go this route, negotiate an agreement with the bank that keeps the foreclosure off your credit report and insist the agreement be put in writing.

The key point of all of the above is that you need to be proactive and not reactive. Your lender will appreciate it and be much more willing to work with you. If you wait for the lender to call you and ask for payment, you're already behind the eight ball and will have to work even harder to get out of your situation.

Here is a list of a few good resources on foreclosure:

- www.youwalkaway.com: This group is located in the heart of foreclosure country (San Diego) and has a great deal of expertise on how to manage the banks, the legal work, and the emotional challenges of foreclosure.

- www.hud.gov/foreclosure/index.cfm: HUD, Department of Housing and Urban Development, is a government agency with some good advice. Its website has contact information for HUD counselors that can help you with your situation.

- www.foreclosurefish.com: Another group that can help you

manage the lender to save your home, or help you through the foreclosure process if required.

Short Sale

In a short sale, you negotiate with the bank to allow you to sell the home for less than is owed, and the bank will eat the difference. A short sale is a great way to sell your house if you have to sell it quickly, and it should be seriously considered before you enter foreclosure. Short sales have become much more common recently, and banks are becoming more receptive to them. There are many firms springing up that specialize in short sales and can help you through the process. Most focus on certain markets, so you should search online for your local market.

Many people wonder why a bank would consider a short sale. From the banks' perspective, there are several reasons why it can be attractive:

- It eliminates the legal costs of foreclosure.

- It reduces the risk of damage to a vacant home.

- The bank makes no mortgage income if the owner defaults.

- Nonperforming loans adversely affect the stock price of the bank.

- Banks have reserve requirements (the amount of cash they're required to keep in their vaults) to meet, and nonperforming loans do not count as an asset toward those requirements.

Warning: A short sale can create credit rating problems and tax issues for the owner. If you are considering a short sale, you should really consult with an attorney, accountant, or other professional who has expertise in this area. A short sale may negatively impact your credit rating if the lender decides to report to the credit agencies that the loan has been settled for less than owed. You should negotiate this issue with the lender when negotiating your deal and request a letter from the lender detailing the situation regarding the short sale. This may reduce the hit your credit rating takes.

Forgiven debt also can create a tax issue. In some cases, tax ramifications can be so significant that they make the sale not worth it. If you owe $300,000 and short-sell the home for $250,000, it creates "debt discharge income" that is a tax liability. The income is taxed as normal income and not capital gains. Because the home was a residence, you're not able to claim a capital gains loss. (If it's an investment rental, you can claim it as a capital gains loss.) Where the real bite comes in is if you bought the home for $200,000, refinanced it several years later for $300,000, then short-sell it for $250,000. In that case, you will have a $50,000 "debt discharge income" for which you will have a full tax burden, *and* you might have to pay the tax on a $50,000 capital gain.

If you go into foreclosure, you will also face the same possible tax consequences. Before you proceed with either path, please get advice from a tax or legal professional. If you cannot afford professional advice, there are many free services available on the web. The last agency you want on your back is the IRS, but there are ways to get forgiveness from them, which a professional can assist you with.

Congress is starting to wake up, and the Mortgage Cancellation Tax Relief Act of 2007 (House Resolution HR 1876) is still working its way through the House Ways and Means Committee.[4] If passed, it will alleviate many of the potential tax issues with short sales and foreclosures. Let's keep our fingers crossed on this one. We all hate paying taxes, but paying taxes on top of losing your home is just adding insult to injury.

CONFRONTING THE EMOTIONS TIED TO YOUR HOME

Corporations have one responsibility, regardless of their rhetoric, and that is to make the most money possible for their shareholders. They will spread whatever misinformation necessary to convince you that the company is right and you, the consumer, are wrong. Mortgage companies, home builders, banks, and Wall Street helped create this mess, but they want the home owner and the taxpayer/government to pay for their greed. They operated out of their own self-interest and created a mass of debt slaves shackled to their homes. You as the home owner need to look out for yourself and your family. If it makes financial sense to walk away from your home, then do it. Just make sure you consult an adviser first.

Buying a home is likely the most emotionally charged purchase you will ever make. It's very difficult to separate the emotions from the correct financial decision. When we decided to sell our home in 2006, it was very hard for me to accept renting and not owning. Moving with two small children was very stressful, especially in the first month after the move. Now that the dust has settled, I cannot begin to tell you how relieved I am that we're renting. We will buy

---

4. I find it fascinating that the government can give Wall Street a trillion dollars in a week, but in a year cannot pass a tax bill that would save homeowners a mere billion in taxes.

another home when the time is right, pay cash for it, and stay in it for a long time.

Too many people allow their emotional relationships with their homes guide their decisions. They say to themselves things like: the market will rebound, the government will do something, and things will turn around soon. The problem is that they often wait until it's too late to make the right decision, pushing themselves into bankruptcy and possibly worse. It is hard to shelve the emotions, but you need to look at your situation objectively and make the wise financial decision. If you don't, it could end up costing you much more down the road.

RECESSION HEAT INDEX			
	SMOKIN' HOT	TEPID	CHILLED
House shopping	Foreclosure auctions	Short sales	Bidding wars
Buying a house	Paying cash	Thirty-year fixed mortgage	Teaser rate
Front yard	$4 worth of veggie seeds	Curb appeal	$12,000 landscaping bill
Florida real estate	$300,000 two-for-one special	$500,000 beach property	$1.2M beach property

7

Disease, Divorce, and Downsizing

Guess What?
The Middle Class Is in Deep Doo-doo

he American middle class is going away, according to Elizabeth Warren, a Harvard law professor, bankruptcy know-it-all, and coauthor of *The Two-Income Trap: Why Middle-Class Mothers and Fathers Are Going Broke*. Soon we will be divided into the haves and the have-nots. In which category will you fall? I assume that if you're reading this book, you want to be in the former group.

WHY IS THE MIDDLE CLASS DISAPPEARING?

WE ARE STRAPPED, COMPARED TO PREVIOUS GENERATIONS, IN FIVE AREAS:

1. We pay 76% more for housing than people did a generation ago (after factoring in inflation), despite low interest rates, and even though the average home is only a tiny bit larger.

2. We pay 74% more for health care.

3. We pay 52% more for cars, but not because cars are more expensive. It's primarily because the median family with two adults now has two cars instead of one.

4. We pay exponentially more for child care, which is a new expense for our generation.

5. We pay 25% more in taxes.

Notice that these five expenses—housing, health care, cars, child care, and taxes—are BIG purchases (as opposed to smaller purchases, like shoes). The second thing to notice is that these purchases are not flexible. It's more difficult to shrink your tax bill, for example, than shrink your landscaping bill. In fact, families spend 75% of their income on these basic five expenses. A generation ago, families spent only 50% of their income on these five expenses.

After these five big expenses are paid every month, today's two-income families with children *actually have less money left over than single parents did just one generation ago.* Families today have less flexibility, more debt, more stress, and a much more difficult time economically.

The Risky Side of the Two-Income Family

The family of today needs two incomes to make it, in contrast to those of a generation ago, when one income was sufficient. The trap that today's two-income family falls into is that they're not living a frugal lifestyle by spending one income and saving the rest as families in other countries do where savings is a priority. (This is partly because saving money and living below one's means is stupidly characterized by our society as a character flaw or old-fashioned. Instead, many families are living a lifestyle that requires two incomes to support. So if one person in the family loses his or her job, then the family won't be able to pay the big car payments, mortgage payment, etc.

One generation ago, families had a person in the wings (usually Mom) who could step in and get a job if the breadwinner (usually Dad) lost his job. She might not have been able to get as high-paying a job as Dad did, but every dollar she brought in was an unbudgeted new dollar. Therefore, those families had a chance of making it and pulling themselves back up to a comfortable financial position. Today's average family has no such luxury. If today's dad loses his job, chances are that the mom is already working, and no one is waiting in the wings to pick up the slack. The income Mom is bringing in is already fully budgeted—in debt obligation (mortgage, car payments, credit cards).

Recession aside, there is also a greater risk of job loss today compared to just one generation ago. This is not taking into account the fact that as the recession progresses, job security is increasingly at stake. So keeping your job today is even more important than before.

HEALTH RISKS

The world of health care has changed. Health insurance covered a five- to ten-day hospital stay for mothers giving birth just one generation ago. Today, mothers are lucky if they're allowed to stay more than twenty-four hours. Thanks, legislators. Sick people get sent home "quicker and sicker," leaving families to perform nursing duties at home, such as washing and irrigating wounds and even giving injections.

With two people working in the household, there is nobody at home to do nurse duty. That means that if somebody gets sick, somebody else has to take off work. As a result, today's family experiences a direct impact on income because of illness. The exploding costs of health insurance have also hit the middle class hard. Insurance is so unaffordable that 48 million working-age American adults went without coverage in 2006.[1] Health insurance is becoming a luxury, with many hardworking Americans forced to make the choice between a mortgage payment and health insurance premiums.

Families in Crisis

How have families been responding to this? Current bankruptcy rates of families with children far exceed bankruptcy rates of single adults or married couples without children. Merely having children puts you at a much higher risk of having to file for bankruptcy. (Feel free to remind little Tyler of this fact after he puts the dog in the dryer.)

Do you know any families who have experienced divorce in the last seven years? Then you actually know even more families who have filed for bankruptcy, statistically. This is because bankruptcy among families with children is now more common than divorce. Every year, there are more children who have to witness their parents' bankruptcy than witness their divorce.

According to Harvard Law School professor Elizabeth Warren, 90% of people who file for bankruptcy file for one of *three big reasons*:

1. Job loss

2. Illness in the family

---

1. Elizabeth Warren, "The New Economics of the Middle Class: Why Making Ends Meet Has Gotten Harder." Testimony before Senate Finance Committee, May 10, 2007.

3. Family breakup: divorce or death

We will examine each of these three areas and discuss how to reduce your chances of having to file for bankruptcy. Preventing any or all of these Big Three will drastically increase your chances of weathering this recession.

Warren claims (and has the data to back this up) that the middle class is disappearing. For the longest time, America's demographic distribution looked like a huge bell curve; we had some poor, some rich, and a gigantic middle class. But now, America is turning into a two-class system: the haves and the have-nots.

There will be a huge increase in the poor class, and also an increase of the "sort of rich" class. The same families with two incomes who don't lose a job, divorce, have a death in the family, or get sick will be thrust into the new "sort of rich" class. The remaining people will be one long trail of underclass, always debt-ridden, and always lacking real economic security.

Simply put, those of us lucky enough to avoid the Big Three will be able to avoid the "have-not" classification.

Why Isn't This all over the News?

The middle class in America has always been seen as boring, or something to make fun of. The middle class isn't as interesting as the poor or the rich, as far as news-making goes. Thus, the issues affecting the middle class have been all but ignored in the media.

What Can I Do about It?

First, ask yourself, will this all depend on luck? Or can some of it be controlled by us? How much of the Big Three can be avoided by planning and making smart personal choices? Let's find out.

Keeping the Breadwinning Job

> *It's a recession when your neighbor loses his job.*
> *It's a depression when you lose your own.*

—Harry Truman

More companies are going to be taking a machete to the employee pool in an attempt to make their bottom lines look better. Unemployment will increase, so make sure it doesn't happen to you, your husband, or whoever is the breadwinner in your household.

Perspective Check from the Great Depression

"I took my baby along to work at the Lucas Cheese factory. He played and slept in a playpen all day long. I'd go over now and then when he fussed to tend to him, but not for long. I was being paid $1.75 a week to work full days and I was fortunate to have a job."

—*Erlenne McColpin, Menomonie, Wisconsin.*

From *Stories and Recipes of the Great Depression of the 1930's* by Rita Van Amber (see Resources).

Be Valuable at Work

Do an honest assessment. Are you among the top 10% of the most-valued employees in your company? Are you vital to its success? To avoid getting laid off, this is where you need to be, as gleaned from the experts:

Rule 1: Never gossip or complain at work, to anyone you work with, or to anyone who knows anyone you work with. I mean *never.* If someone asks you how you are, you respond, "Great. How are you doing?" Even if your boss has an "open door" policy, he or she seriously does not want to hear your tales of woe. Bosses are stressed out enough as it is because revenues are down. The last thing you need is to give them an excuse to ax your job, so keep your mouth shut and put on a happy face.

Rule 2: Don't pout. This goes along with Rule 1. Studies show that 70% of human communication is nonverbal. What is your body language saying? Are you hunched over? Are your shoes off or your feet propped up on the desk? That body language screams "lazy" and will get you thrown out faster than a gun-toting drunk at the White House (unless you're Dick Cheney). Sit up straight, look people in the eye, and be polite and courteous.

Rule 3: Get to work early and stay late. You need to spend more time working, but not necessarily getting more work done. Many times, it's unclear how much an employee produces, but start time and end time are indisputable. Bosses notice when you come and when you leave. If you can swing it, come in before your boss arrives, and leave after. This creates the illusion that you are hard at work and always producing, when in fact all it proves is that you're *there.* Send an e-mail to your team, and copy your boss, at 1:00 in the morning. Your boss will be impressed that you're hard at work while all his other lazy employees are sleeping. But in fact, you're just working hard to keep your job.

Rule 4: Stand on your own. Don't firmly attach yourself to others, especially office cliques. The idea is to be seen as independent, thus reducing your chance of getting cut because of your association to others on the chopping block. Don't get too close to your boss, either. If she gets canned, you don't want to go with her.

Rule 5: Take a salary cut. I know, this sounds about as much fun as "summering" at a POW camp. If jobs are getting slashed all around you, and your company is in trouble, offer to take a salary cut. Tell your boss that it's fine, you'll manage to "just get by with less for a while."

Rule 6: Act like you're grateful for your job. Repeat to yourself, "I am happy to be working. I am lucky to have income," as your daily mantra. It's okay that your coworker gets to go on a boondoggle in Hawaii while you have to stay back at the office. It's fine that you had to spend the entire weekend refining your boss's proposal. It's all great, because you have income and you're keeping your job.

Rule 7: Don't make personal calls or send personal e-mails on the job. Alleged use of company phones and e-mail systems for personal use is easily provable. Don't make yourself vulnerable to a petty, backstabbing coworker complaining that you're guilty of such acts. When times get tough, people play dirty, so protect yourself.

Rule 8: Don't sleep with your coworkers or show up hungover . . . At least not until the recession is over.

Rule 9: Make friends with higher-ups. Ask them for advice, and offer to get involved (even in a small way) with projects to which you have not been assigned. Volunteer for charities the company or the executives are involved with. Expanding your work network, especially among the decision makers, is vital.

Rule 10: Do or create something valuable. Go above and beyond in some way, on something that either saves your company money or increases revenue. Be on the lookout for glaring inefficiencies and think of clever ways to eliminate them.

Rule 11: Toot your own horn to the people who matter. Take credit for results that you produced. Do it in a nonegocentric and polite way (but do it before someone else takes the credit for you).

Oops, I Lost My Job. Now What?

If you do lose your breadwinning job, you're not alone. Market jitters, a declining dollar, and general economic upheaval are sending unemployment on an upward trend. More and more people will be losing their jobs, so try not to take it personally. Allow yourself a brief period of time to wallow in self-pity (at least five minutes, but no more than a day), and then get going to find another breadwinning job right away.

The silver lining to the cloud of unemployment is the beautiful cushion of overseas job opportunities, thanks to globalization. Job opportunities abroad for families with a sense of adventure and cultural appreciation will abound. Working abroad can be fun, rewarding, and a great way to fast-track your career. So, why not try living abroad for three years? The reasons are many for considering a job overseas.

- Working abroad might provide better job security for the next several years. While U.S. companies are cutting back and downsizing, reduced revenues will also translate into few or no raises for the people who remain. Growth companies abroad will be hiring, and offering more financial incentives to employees.

- The job skills of people with U.S. business experience are in high demand in emerging economies around the world. And while the economy in the United States slows, there is still continued growth in emerging markets such as China, India, Brazil, Russia, and the Middle East.

- Inflation and the declining value of the dollar make it cheaper for foreign companies to hire U.S. workers, as other currencies like the euro, the Chinese yuan, and the Brazilian real are comparatively stronger.

- Working overseas is a great way to beef up your résumé. When the U.S. economy rebounds, you will be in an excellent position to climb the ranks back at home. International work experience is rare and highly valued by U.S. companies.

- It could be one of the most rewarding experiences of your life. Most people and families who chose to live abroad returned to the U.S. having experienced personal growth, fun stories to share, and other benefits from the adventure.

Keeping Illness Away

Thou shouldst eat to live; not live to eat.

—Socrates

The U.S. health care system is broken, to say the least. We have some of the best doctors in the world, yet nearly 50 million Americans do not have health insurance, and Americans are sicker than ever. The World Health Organization says the United States' health system ranks a measly number 37 worldwide.

The key to a healthier lifestyle involves taking responsibility for your health and taking proactive steps to achieve it. Prevention is definitely the best medicine, and if you or a family member are already sick, you need to do everything in your power to reverse illness. It's your body, so take responsibility for it. Our health care system will not take care of it for you.

Depression-era women instinctively knew that proper nutrition was the key to surviving and to maintaining good health. They didn't have vitamin supplements, personal trainers, or advice from nutritionists. Yet in countless Great Depression stories I've read, they made nutrition for their families the highest priority. When it comes down to it, what does one have if not good health?

If you want to read a convincing, well-researched book on the distinct link between nutrition and disease reversal and prevention, pick up Dr. Joel Fuhrman's[2] *Eat to Live: The Revolutionary Formula for Fast and Sustained Weight Loss.* Dr. Fuhrman and Dr. Mehmet Oz (a frequent guest on *Oprah*)

---

2. Joel Fuhrman, M.D., is a family physician, a graduate of the University of Pennsylvania School of Medicine, and a member of the Board of Directors of the National Health Association. He is one of the leading experts on nutrition and natural healing, and has appeared on television shows and networks including CNN, ABC, CBS, FOX, *Today*, *Good Morning America*, CNBC, and many more.

have been colleagues for years and share similar philosophies on nutrition and disease. The information in this section is gleaned from their exhaustive research, specifically Dr. Fuhrman's.

THE TWO BIG KILLERS: CANCER AND HEART DISEASE

Everybody knows that there is a huge body of evidence that proves high cholesterol levels (measured in milligrams per deciliter of blood) are linked to heart disease. Specifically, the risk of heart disease proportionately increases as cholesterol increases over 150mg/dL. By and large, people who have cholesterol below 150mg/dL *do not have heart attacks*, as the Framingham Heart Study found. Most heart attacks occur in people who have cholesterol levels between 175 and 225.

In rural China, where the average cholesterol level is 127, only 5% of the people ever suffer a heart attack. In shocking contrast, 40% of Americans *die* of heart attacks. Why is this? Well, as the famous China-Cornell-Oxford Project (one of the largest epidemiological studies done anywhere at any time) found, it has to do with nutrition. People in rural China consume a simple, plant-based diet and rarely consume animal products. Americans eat processed foods out of a box, fast food, tons of animal products, and only small amounts of high-nutrient foods, like spinach.

Based on Dr. Fuhrman's research, if you want to put yourself and your family at *zero* risk of heart disease, you need to change your food habits. Get the majority of your calories from whole foods with a high nutrition content—beans, vegetables, fruits, seeds, and nuts. There is no magical drug that will provide the same results. In fact, the cholesterol drugs have nasty side effects, and the toxicity from these drugs themselves causes disease.

Can you prevent cancer? According to Dr. Fuhrman, who has spent the last twenty years reviewing more than 60,000 scientific articles analyzing the relationship between cancer and diet and nutrition, the short answer is yes, much of the time. On his website, Dr. Fuhrman states that 85% of all cancer is caused by environmental and lifestyle factors such as a diet high in processed food and low in fruits and vegetables, chemicals in our foods (additives), environmental pollution, drugs, and medical procedures. Treating disease is an enormously profitable business, and in order to secure more and more funding for drug treatments and cancer therapies, the medical establishment promises that a cure is just around the corner. Despite the fact that over $20 billion of research money has gone to find a cancer cure in the last ten years, the death rate from cancer has only declined 1% per year since 2004.[3]

Fiji Islanders smoke like chimneys, yet rarely get lung cancer. Hawaii residents smoke much less but get lung cancer in droves. How can this be? Because the chain-smoking Fijians are protected by the massive amounts of green vegetables they consume. Diabetes, stroke, arthritis, and a host of other diseases are also preventable, as well as reversible.

---

3. FOXNews, "After Years of Declines, Cancer Death Rate Increases," February 20, 2008. www.foxnews.com/story/0,2933,331409,00.html.

Perspective Check from the Great Depression

" 'Vitamins' was not a word in the dictionary. We knew instinctively that unless we served a variety of foods, our families would not be well."

—H. C.

From *Stories and Recipes of the Great Depression of the 1930's* by Rita Van Amber (see Resources).

The Magical Greens and Beans Diet

In a nutshell, an antidisease diet looks like this:

Unrestricted quantities of fruit
Unrestricted quantities of green vegetables
Starchy vegetables in moderation
Whole grains in moderation
Unrestricted quantities of beans
Nuts and seeds in limited amounts

Another way to put this:

- 30–70% of your calories should come from vegetables and beans.

- 20–50% of your calories should come from fruit.

- 5–20% of your calories should come from seeds, nuts, and whole grains.

- Eat fish twice a week or less.

- Eat fat-free dairy twice a week or less.

- Eat eggs, oils, and poultry once weekly or less.

- Rarely eat red meat, sweets, cheese, milk, processed foods, or hydrogenated oils.

If this type of diet sounds hard-core, that's because it is. Make no mistake about it—it is vastly different from the average American diet. But the average American is sick. Do you want to be average or healthy?

To many, eating this way would be unrealistic. But would it kill you to eat like this even 50% of the time? If so, at least consider adding more beans and greens to your regular diet.

If we could give every individual the right amount of nourishment and exercise, not too little and not too much, we would have found the safest way to health.

—Hippocrates

Organic or Conventional Produce?

There are many reasons to eat organic produce. Some people think it tastes better, and it is better for farmers and the environment. Some studies even claim that organic produce has a higher flavonoid content (an antioxidant).

However, there is an enormous amount of research that supports the fact that consumption of produce, organic or not, protects against disease and is related to lower cancer risk. Eating any type of produce greatly outweighs any risks associated with pesticide consumption. You wouldn't drive your car without wearing a seat belt because it might wrinkle your shirt, would you? Well, don't abstain from produce because you think the pesticides are bad for you. Eat the produce anyway, and buy organic whenever you can (or grow your own).

THE ONLY PROVEN WAY TO INCREASE LONGEVITY

There is only one way to increase your lifespan. It's called caloric restriction. There is a huge body of evidence—enormous, irrefutable, and across all species tested (from insects to humans)—that supports this. Lean people live longer. Every pound of extra fat you carry on your body brings increased risk of diseases like cancer, heart disease, diabetes, and high blood pressure.

CAN YOU PINCH AN INCH?

Forget BMI (body mass index). BMI doesn't give you enough information, and it can incorrectly label heavily muscled people as "obese." For example, take tennis goddess Serena Williams, with her incredibly healthy, muscular 5'9" frame. Let's calculate her BMI.

$$BMI = \text{weight in pounds} \times 703 \div \text{height}^2 \text{ in inches}$$

$$\text{Serena's BMI} = 165 \times 703 \div 69^2 = 24.36$$

A BMI over 24 would incorrectly categorize Serena as overweight. The preceding calculation was based on her weight being 165 pounds, a rough estimation, but it still shows that BMI calculations are flawed when used as a basis for judging health.

A better way, according to Fuhrman, is to look at body fat. Pinch the skin around your tummy. Women should have no more than an inch to pinch, while men should have no more than half an inch to pinch. Statistically, even an extra ten pounds puts us at increased risk of health problems. And most people who don't think they carry too much fat actually do. I'm still in the process of Mission Belly Fat Eradication. Every bit helps and it does take time, so be patient and kind to yourself. The Japanese are taking the belly fat war seriously. Due to their rapidly increasing rates of diabetes and heart disease, they have instituted a national law that requires everyone between the ages of forty and seventy-four to get an annual waist measurement. Companies and local governments will be fined if their employees don't meet target waist measurement goals. Japanese citizens are so concerned they're using their cell phones to take photos of meals and sending them to nutritionists for analysis.

> *Nothing will benefit human health and increase*
> *chances for survival of life on Earth as much*
> *as the evolution to a vegetarian diet.*
>
> —*Albert Einstein*

STAYING TOGETHER

> *If a man is in the forest, and there*
> *isn't a woman around, is he still wrong?*
>
> —*Bumper sticker*

Recessions and bear markets always cause increases in divorce rates. Any time a sudden increase or decrease in income occurs, there is an increased risk of divorce, Keren Blankfeld Schultz noted in a Forbes online article (July 7, 2008). If you are married or partnered and you share finances, then you should focus on staying together and strengthening your relationship. If things are rocky and you are contemplating a divorce/breakup, be aware that now is not an opportune time to do so. Except in cases of really ugly marital situations (like abuse), divorce is often devastating for women—especially if young children are involved. Divorce not only causes emotional heartache but for women can also be financially devastating. And so can a recession, so let's not add insult to injury (if you can avoid it).

Women, not men, initiate more than two-thirds of all divorces. The most common reason that women file for divorce has nothing to do with the ugly stuff, such as abuse or addiction or neglect. Rather, the principal issue is "lack of connection," according to psychiatrist Scott Haltzman, author of *The Secrets of Happily Married Men: Eight Ways to Win Your Wife's Heart Forever.*

If you do have a legitimate reason to get a divorce, and it absolutely cannot be avoided, you should approach the situation as a negotiator, not a fighter. Fighting equals mammoth legal bills. Don't give up your hard-earned cash to the attorneys. Be civil and negotiate. You can minimize the legal bills this way, and both of you will be richer at the end.

Perspective Check from the Great Depression

"We were married in 1933 and our furniture was mostly orange crates. But I believe we were more happy and had more love than today."

—*Phyllis Schroeder, Menomonie, Wisconsin.*

From *Stories and Recipes of the Great Depression of the 1930's* by Rita Van Amber (see Resources).

Recessions can bring new meaning to the concept of "ugly divorce." The most substantial marital asset is usually a home, and dividing a home equitably is very tricky these days. When more is owed on a home than it's worth, the threat of foreclosure looms large on the man or woman left holding the "asset" (really debt).

A Texas mother of two was recently interviewed by *Forbes* magazine. Her husband had walked out on her, leaving her with an unaffordable mortgage payment that her job at a preschool simply could not support. She ended up negotiating a short sale of the home with the bank, and eventually moved to a rented apartment.

In recent years, talk of divorce included the rundown on how to divvy up assets. Now the talk inclines more to how the losses are split up, who is responsible for the credit card debt, and who will be paying off the mortgage.

THE SECRET OF A LASTING MARRIAGE

According to Dr. Cheryl McClary, women's health professor and author of *The Commitment Chronicles: The Power of Staying Together*, the key to a lasting marriage is for women to understand themselves and be emotionally whole. Women waste their time trying to change their men, because it's impossible. We can change and control only ourselves—nobody else.

Once you focus on yourself, find true love for yourself, and shift your focus away from your husband, amazing things will start to happen in your relationship. The whole dynamic can begin to shift, because you've placed yourself in a leadership position, instead of that of a follower. To help yourself and to love yourself are the simple keys.

This philosophy fits very well into the theme of the book you're reading: how women can control their destinies, financially and otherwise.

DO NOT ALLOW ANOTHER WOMAN
TO STEAL YOUR MAN

During a weak economy, expect that your man will be hit on by other women with alarming frequency. The vultures will be hungry and looking for a meal ticket from any man with a pulse and a steady income. Suddenly, the things you find annoying, like his beer gut and ball-scratching habit, will be labeled "cute" by some floozy on the hunt. Think that his wedding ring will deter this type of attention? Most of my married male friends claim that, ironically, they get hit on more while wearing it. To the vultures, his wedding ring doesn't say, "I'm married, stay away." It says, "I'm stable, not afraid of commitment, and probably not a crack addict."

A man with a stressful job, a busy schedule, and no free time might look at an affair almost as a vacation—a welcome relief from the everyday. Chances are, he's looking to have some fun, not to intentionally hurt you. So try to keep this in perspective.

Technology has added an extra element to affairs because people can literally chat all day long. This makes the woman with whom he's having the affair accessible around the clock, at least on the emotional/flirtation level. Again, this provides an escape from the man's everyday life, adds excitement, and does not require much effort on his part.

Stay alert and aware of your husband's whereabouts, his social schedule, and with whom he associates. I'm not advocating obsessive hovering, just awareness. Pay attention to him and your relationship, and make time for just the two of you.

Consider the following tidbits, reported by Nancy Polk in a *New York Times* interview with Dr. Janis Abrahms Spring (November 15, 1998):

- Fear of sexually transferred diseases has not resulted in a decline in affairs.
- An affair over the computer is still an affair and a violation of trust.
- Roughly 1 in every 2.6 married people have an affair at some point.
- Big swings in income, up or down, result in increased occurrences of affairs.
- Religion does not keep people from having affairs; rules and guilt do not prevent affairs.

If, God forbid, Mr. Wonderful waltzes through the door one day and announces that he's leaving you for his personal assistant/the nanny/the local barista/his tennis coach/your best friend, keep your cool. Then you really must put your foot down, especially if this is a first-time offense. I'm not excusing his behavior, but clueless men in a moment of weakness can easily be manipulated by a hungry she-wolf. Think about it—the type of woman who will not only solicit an affair with your husband but also try to steal him must be in a desperate position. She will stop at nothing to get your man, and probably has nothing to lose. She must be stopped, and the affair must be stopped. Really, it's a lot quicker, easier, and less financially devastating than divorce.

According to Dr. Spring, author of *After the Affair: Healing the Pain and Rebuilding Trust When a Partner Has Been Unfaithful* and clinical supervisor of Yale's psychology department, affairs that are forbidden are hot. For him, the euphoria and intoxication make it seem like the affair is "true love," like the other woman is the soul mate, like she is the answer to all his prayers. At this point, the man is, for all intents and purposes, crazy "in love" and willing to sacrifice everything for the other woman, no matter how reckless or irresponsible his behavior might be. Often, the men can't even explain their behavior (that's how out of their minds they are).

The thing about crazy love is that time reveals that it's not true love. That is why I suggest putting your foot down at this point. It's just like doing an intervention for a friend you think is falling off a cliff (and into alcohol, drugs, or something else). You're going to have to be the sane person who intervenes.

Dr. Spring believes the one key thing that must be present to reestablish trust and start forgiveness is compassion from the offending party for the hurt he caused. Additionally, the cheater, going forward, needs to go out of his way to make the other person feel safe. It takes time for the hurt party to heal, and it takes work from both parties.

If you try to work through this situation together, you might be rewarded with a stronger marriage in the end. He'll spend the rest of his life in awe of how strong and forgiving you are and how lucky he is, and he'll be making it up to you forever. And even if the forgiveness path doesn't work out for you and you end up divorcing him, at least you can walk away knowing that you gave it a shot and tried to work things out.

When Hillary Clinton forgave Bill, there was public outrage (mostly from women) that she let him off the hook too easily. The media were all over the story, questioning her dignity and feminist ideals. As if she wasn't dealing with enough at the time, the press added mudslinging to her woes. We all know what happened next. She rose above it—way above it—ran for president, and put the whole mess behind her. The point is, our society may look down upon women who forgive a cheating spouse. But who cares what other people think? It's your marriage, not theirs. Don't put yourself in the victim role. It's demeaning and can cloud your judgment. Whether you decide to forgive or move on, you'll still have your dignity intact.

	SMOKIN' HOT	TEPID	CHILLED
Vacation	Staying home to save your job	Disney World	Summering in the French Riviera
Marriage	Getting his flirtatious secretary fired	Staying together for the kids	Divorce
Work perks	Thanking God every day for your job	Employee loyalty programs	Signing bonuses
Peak Oil	Bike to work	Bus to work	85-mile commute
Trendy job	Debt collector	Recruiter	Mortgage broker/ Realtor

RECESSION HEAT INDEX

8

Letting Go of the Cool Factor

Buying Less Junk and Embracing the Authentic

o you ever wonder why spending money holds such great appeal for women? We don't *go* shopping so much as *are* shopping. All the time. Like a moth to a flame, the hypnotic cycle of work, shop, and spend sucks us in, burns us, and then spits us out.

Don't get me wrong, I love shopping on occasion, especially when it masquerades as a social adventure with my girlfriends or family. And yes, I have stuff. I am not a person whose possessions total two pairs of pants, a wheatgrass juicer, and a sustainably farmed wood coffee table. I'm coming clean right now: I have a fondness for stuff. Especially stuff that's been beautifully designed with actual *thought* behind it. Buying books, lipsticks, shoes, or whatever, gives me a tiny thrill. Sometimes the process of hunting and buying is more exhilarating than the stuff itself. Oh, and I love to look good. I'm

vain. Do not ever ask me to part with my beauty products.
Ever.

Okay, so now that I've outed myself as a narcissistic brainwashed consumer, there is another side to this story. I don't
live to shop anymore. I can't put my finger on exactly when I
lost my intense desire to shop all the time, but I suspect it has
something to do with the countless hours I spent as a bored
teenager hanging out at the mall for entertainment. Perhaps
my system reached a saturation point, overloaded by the fluo-
rescent lighting, stale air, bass-heavy hip-hop pounding in my
ears, and an endless array of choices. The mall is a sensory
overload. At some point, it also became evident that, quite
frankly, there are much better things to do with my time than
shop. So now shopping is like doing tequila shots—something
I do when necessary and in moderation.

I suspect that my distaste for shopping will serve me and
my family well during the economic storm on the horizon. I
worry, though, about people stuck in shopping's "vise grip."
What kind of emotional and financial devastation are they
heading for? None, if they are ridiculously rich and can afford
to keep up the habit. Unfortunately, most of us do not fall into
this category, and there will be a rude awakening.

Ridding yourself of your addiction to stuff and no longer
blowing money that you don't have will give you such a feeling of liberation. Minimize, and find joy in the simple things
in life. If you are able to adopt a new mind-set about shopping
and buying, then you will be able to sail through a recession
(or depression) much easier.

PERSPECTIVE CHECK FROM
THE GREAT DEPRESSION

"Clothes came from wherever we could get them, such as older rags that were big enough to get pieces from. Our undertaker in town used to bring us clothes that people would get rid of when people died. We made blankets and whatever we could out of material that was usable. We also raised a couple of pigs for our winter sausage. When we look back at these times, we feel they were the best times of our lives because we had to work things out ourselves as a family and made our own amusement."

—Mrs. E. Hart, Oak Creek, Wisconsin.

From *Stories and Recipes of the Great Depression of the 1930's* by Rita Van Amber (see Resources).

WHY WE SPEND

Ultimately, we can thank the corporations that spend billions to brainwash us into thinking that a shiny new thing is better than an old or used thing, and that purchasing will make us happy and attract friends and lovers into our lives. The scheme has been well orchestrated, affecting our entire culture and psychology.

ADVERTISERS

What is a psychographic, and will it make me hallucinate? Psychographics is the study of lifestyle, desires, and your personal outlook on the world. Advertisers spend billions trying to decipher your buying habits, and marketers take the data and use it to determine specific psychological triggers that make you buy. Dirty trick, this is.

SHOPPING AS A SOCIAL/ENTERTAINMENT OUTLET

The U.S. has three times more square footage of retail space per person than Western Europe. Shopping is usually not as simple as finding what you need, purchasing it, and then going home. Shopping centers are designed to invite people in and keep them there for long periods of time. Marketing research has concluded that most purchases occur during the third hour of shopping. So the retailers' goal is to keep you there for three hours. This is accomplished by setting up the shopping environment to be winding and inviting, with lots of pleasant aromas. That creates the perfect setting for either hanging out with friends and family or shopping by yourself. You meet a friend at the mall because you want to be together, and because the mall makers have created a shiny, colorful, entertaining habitat for the two of you.

MEDIA

Popular television shows and movies pound us with images of a lifestyle that is unattainable and unrealistic. While it seems like watching these shows gives us a break from reality, they are actually serving up self-doubt about our own personal levels of success. Those who get sucked in and attempt to keep up with these "cool" lifestyles end up overspending and sinking into credit card debt.

So Many Choices, So Affordable

Goods that were once considered luxury items are now affordable, if not a bargain, for most people. Cheap but tasteful retailers offer low prices and an apparent healthy alternative to the conspicuous consumption of, say, shopping at Barneys. The popularity of stores like Old Navy, Target, and IKEA has exploded because they seem to offer good stuff at cheap prices. But the cheapness may distract us from the fact that many of these products are pretty crappy and fall apart. The products might cost less, but we're replacing them faster.

The other major seduction in the cheap retail game is to make us feel we can "afford" to buy in multiples. Like those shorts on sale? Hell, why not buy them in three different colors? Before you know it, your trip to the store for toilet paper and deodorant ends with a full shopping cart and a $300 tab.

Out-of-control inflation in coming years will bring the cheap retail model to a grinding halt. Expect that things will no longer be cheap for us Americans as prices (even at Wal-Mart) climb steadily. Foreigners traveling here, however, will be delighted at how cheap everything seems because their currency will be strong against the U.S. dollar.

Easy Credit

If your mailbox is anything like ours, it is stuffed daily with credit card offers. Today almost anyone who desires a credit card can get one, including teenagers, admitted drug addicts, and welfare recipients. The credit card companies, offering enticing bonus APRs, balance transfers, and pretty personalization options, lure us into debt in exchange for the promise of emotional satisfaction. They enable people to keep up with the lifestyles they want but cannot afford.

The "Because I Deserve It" Syndrome

When you're feeling crappy, depressed, or even just bored, shopping mentally wraps you in a blanket and gives you a warm cup of tea. Emotional shoppers often feel entitled, as if they deserve to buy something because some circumstance warrants the expense. Emotional shoppers shop when they . . .

Are tired or bored
Had a fight with a loved one
Received good or bad news
Need a break from the kids
Hear someone say, "You can't take it with you"
Are seeking revenge against their spouse
Notice that everyone else does it
See it's sunny outside
Had to suck it up and work all weekend
Are too tired to go to the gym
Don't feel like doing the laundry
Feel that they are a good person

Do any of the above seem familiar to you? Emotional shopping is one of the quickest ways to find yourself in debt. According to Jerrold Mundis in *How to Get Out of Debt, Stay Out of Debt, and Live Prosperously,* when shopping is used as a substitute for love, as a reward, or to ease anxiety, debt soon follows. The antidote to emotional shopping is keeping an expense record (see Expense Tracking with Chinese Water Torture, page 77).

Family and Friends

Although you might not realize it, there is often tremendous pressure from family and friends to spend money. Whether they apply that pressure through direct nagging or more indirect means, the end result is the same. Saying no is very difficult to do, and fear of disappointing friends or family leads to overspending.

Spending money on trips, meals out, or shopping excursions with your family can be loads of fun, but looking at the credit card bill afterward can be brutal. Next time you find yourself getting caught in this trap, ask yourself if there is some alternative. Can you show my love in a different way that doesn't cost much? Can you go on a long walk together instead of talking over a $50 steak?

BRANDED KIDS

If you asked a parent in the 1940s, "What do you want for your children more than anything else?" the answer would likely be, "I want to raise my child to have a strong character." Fast-forward to today. If you ask any parent that question now, the overwhelming response would be, "I want my child to be happy." Well, the marketing geniuses have convinced parents that happiness is something that can be bought. As a result, parents spend more money on their children, as a percentage of income, than at any other time in history. Why? Because according to James McNeal,[1] an expert who has done decades of research on kids' marketing, parents are forking over their paychecks to satisfy their children's wants (not needs), primarily to "make them happy." When you give in to your children's consumption desires, you are no longer in control of your money. They are. This firmly plants the children at the top of the family hierarchy, holding the reins of the money horse. Scary.

---

1. In Cynthia Kopkowski, "From Legos to Logos." *NEA Today* (National Education Association), May 2006.

Take a stroll down the halls of any middle or high school in America and you will witness enthusiastic displays of consumerism everywhere. Juicy Couture sweatshirts ($100), 7 for All Mankind designer jeans ($150), iPods ($300), and cell phones are everywhere. The conspicuous display of logos is evidence of the hollow pursuit of securing one's social status and a seat at the lunchroom cool table. According to Alissa Quart (*Branded: The Buying and Selling of Teenagers*), children use brands to define their world. They fabricate an image of themselves using money and brands as primary tools.

Don't think that only tweens and teens fall victim to the brand brainwashing campaign. Children are marketed to from infancy. Two-year-olds are now able to recognize brands and are quick to demand them (usually in a high-pitched whine at the supermarket).

Take note: You are not doing your children any favors—and certainly are not providing them with true happiness—by paying for their $60 a month phone bill, or caving in to that Puma shoe purchase. You're merely fueling the brand machine, which in turn distorts your child's ambitions, self-image, and views on your own community. In short, you are reducing your child's value system to the lowest common denominator by buying, *literally*, into this game.

PERSPECTIVE CHECK FROM THE GREAT DEPRESSION

"My parents were middle class farmers when they started. Then the depression came and it changed all that. We wore our shoes out with big holes in the soles, so we'd put fresh cardboard in every morning before leaving for school. We all wore the same dresses at school. They were made out of feed bags and only one neighbor had a pattern. So we all used the same pattern with the same rickrack around the neck, sleeves, and hems."

—Gwen Manske, Menomonie, Wisconsin.

From *Stories and Recipes of the Great Depression of the 1930's* by Rita Van Amber (see Resources).

LIVING SIMPLY, WITH TASTE

Whether you remove yourself from the marketing machine now in preparation for the recession, or during the depths of it out of necessity, is up to you. The benefit of doing it now is that you will have taken responsible steps to prepare you and your family for unsettling times.

CLOTHES SHOPPING THE PRACTICAL, CHIC WAY

The goal here is to give up the quest for stuff you don't need. Focus instead on buying things that are made with a degree of decent quality (stuff that lasts a long time, has timeless style, and that you will enjoy for years to come). Avoid all the disposable and trendy items that are tempting today but will be shoved into the back of a closet somewhere within four months.

Think about Audrey Hepburn's style. She always dressed well and looked gorgeous, and if she were to hop off the *Breakfast at Tiffany's* set and walk down the street today, she would still look modern, cool, and beautiful. Her style was timeless. She didn't give in to every hot trend. She knew her own body and how to dress to flatter it. She had her own individual style and didn't give a crap about what other people were doing. That is chic defined.

Shop for quality items that you will use frequently and love for years to come. The goal should not be accumulation but instead thoughtful selection.

The Story of the Red Coat

In 1997, I set out to find a winter coat. Something to stave off the drizzly cold Seattle winter and keep me warm and cozy like a swaddled baby. The perfect coat is not easy to find. In fact, during this particular shopping excursion, I must have spent three hours driving, perusing, consolidating, and trying on coats of all types. From fluffy, oversized, down-filled parkas to fur-lined, sherpa, and leather, I left no style unturned.

Suddenly, like a beacon of light shining amidst a sea of beige, I spotted a crimson wool coat with simple, clean lines, a feminine cut, and unbridled style. It was not expensive, but it looked well made (in the U.S.A.), and the fit was perfect. I took it home, enjoyed it all winter, and sadly put it away when the warm weather returned.

From a cost-per-usage perspective, this coat was one of the smartest purchases I have ever made. I still look forward to wearing it every winter. People still stop me on the street to ask, "Where did you get that coat?" The experience of owning this gem really changed my perspective on shopping and the value of having something you love versus something you bought to pass the time (or that happened to be on sale).

Shopping Less . . . Now What?

Your new shopping diet might leave you with a surprising amount of free time. Between driving, parking, browsing, waiting in line to check out, driving home again, unpacking the car, disposing of the packaging, and hiding the indulgence from your husband (and/or arguing about it), buying stuff takes a lot of time.

Go forth and do something else with your time. Anything, really, other than shopping. What would happen if the countless hours women spend shopping were spent doing something creative, constructive, or civic-minded?

Choosing a simpler lifestyle presents you with a great opportunity for you to live better and become better. Learn a foreign language, play a new sport, start a business, create a second income, join a stitch-and-bitch club, meditate . . . your options are endless. Fill the void by replacing your old consumer habits with new, better, fun habits.

RECESSION HEAT INDEX			
	SMOKIN' HOT	TEPID	CHILLED
Philosophy	Downmarket	Value conscious	Upmarket
Passing the time	Chess	Recreational shopping	Binge buying
Clothing	Secondhand	Generic brand	Designer labels
Shopping	craigslist	eBay	Paying retail

9

How to Get Stuff Cheap

Getting What You Need Creatively

This recession does not have to diminish your lifestyle if you already have positive cash flow and savings in the bank. For more information on investments that can help offset inflation and subsidize your mani/pedi habit, please see the last chapter, "Where We Stuffed Our Money."

For those with debt and for those who simply want to consume less, spend less money, and save more, this chapter is for you. Even if you're currently at break-even every month, reducing your expenses can help you build your financial cushion or put it in recession-proof investments that could really pay off once the storm has passed.

PERSPECTIVE CHECK FROM THE GREAT DEPRESSION

"Those were frugal days, but they left us with a happy childhood."

—*J. Tamse, New Berlin, Wisconsin.*

From *Stories and Recipes of the Great Depression of the 1930's* by Rita Van Amber (see Resources).

FOOD

EATING ON THE CHEAP

Food bills account for a large part of most American spending, so we'll start here. The most obvious ways to save on food are:

- Don't eat out or buy food on the run. Plan in advance and pack food if you're going to be out all day.

- Buy only whole foods, not commercially processed stuff. Think old-fashioned oatmeal instead of boxed cereal.

- Do not buy anything individually packaged, including juice boxes or snack-size cracker packets.

- Shop and plan meals around foods that are amazingly cheap and nutritious, like beans.

PERSPECTIVE CHECK FROM THE GREAT DEPRESSION

"In all of this, I have one most important duty—that my family grows up with the best possible nourishment I can provide. Our health must come first."

—H. Circhy, Millerville, Minnesota.

From *Stories and Recipes of the Great Depression of the 1930's* by Rita Van Amber (see Resources).

BUYING IN BULK

If you really want to get serious about slashing your food budget, I recommend buying food in bulk. Bulk shopping can save you time and money in the long term. Obviously, fresh foods purchased in bulk must be consumed quickly, or prepared and frozen. But many foods with a long shelf life can be stored in your home for long periods. You might need to get clever if you don't have a lot of storage space. I've heard of people stashing bulk items under beds, in closets, or in the garage.

FREEZE AND SAVE

Purchasing a chest freezer is the next step toward dramatically reducing your food bills. Even if you live in an apartment and are short on space, you can buy a freezer with a lock on it and request permission to leave it in a common area, such as the basement.

Chest freezer, how do I love thee? Let me count the ways.

We purchased ours for about $100 when I started pureeing veggies and making baby food for my first baby. Soon after, I started stuffing my freezer with yummy homemade stews, pancakes, and meals ready to go at a moment's notice. There are many names for this time- and money-saving technique: batch cooking, freezer cooking, OAMC (once-a-month cooking), meal assembly, and my personal favorite—mega-cooking.

Here is a partial list of foods and meals that freeze really well:

Chili, soups, and stews, with or without meat
Sauces
Bean and lentil soups
Tomato-based dishes, like lasagna
Pancakes, muffins, quick breads, and waffles
Cheese-stuffed pasta shells
Blanched vegetables
Meat, fish, and poultry
Very firm cooked pasta

  Foods that don't freeze well:

Rice dishes (unless suspended in liquid)
Potato dishes
Veggies with high moisture content
Greasy or fried foods

  There are many benefits of batch cooking. First, the convenience of it is unmatched. It's great to have a freezer full of delicious, healthy food at the ready. There's no need to rush home after a busy day and prepare something from scratch. I also love the freedom of being able to invite friends over at the last minute for a tasty lunch or dinner, knowing that all of the work has been done and all I have to do is defrost and heat. I typically keep at least three or four different kinds of soup on hand, and muffins or scones. Toss up a quick salad, and presto, it's a party. Second, batch cooking is really cheap. Buying the ingredients in bulk dramatically reduces the cost per serving. Take soups. First of all, most canned soups are crap, but let's put that aside for a moment to examine the financial angle. A 10-ounce can of disgusting, chemical-infested bean and ham soup at the supermarket will cost you roughly $1.80. Homemade spicy lentil chicken soup will run you closer to $0.40 per 10-ounce serving. Hmmm . . . which should you choose? The steaming cancer in a bowl, or the aromatic restaurant-quality cuisine for 75% less?

My freezer addiction was fueled by my love of cheap and exquisite food and my lack of free time. I simply never had the time to cook a big family meal every night. So I scoured various online recipe sources like www.epicurious.com, and various cookbooks, to find great recipes that would also freeze well. Now there are entire cookbooks devoted to this method of cooking, and even franchise businesses like Dinners Ready! to cater to those interested in learning batch-cooking skills and outsourcing some of the work involved.

PERSPECTIVE CHECK FROM THE GREAT DEPRESSION

"Nothing was thrown away—we ate what was fixed. We never said 'yuk' about food or we would have been disciplined."

—*Alma Smith, Woodville, Wisconsin.*

From *Stories and Recipes of the Great Depression of the 1930's* by Rita Van Amber (see Resources).

Shopping Smart for Food

It's time to rethink your weekly (or, for some people, daily) pilgrimage to the grocery store. There are cheaper alternatives that offer quality as good or better. Ask your thrifty friends and neighbors where they shop. You might discover a real gem for your food needs. Explore the following:

Local stores that specialize in natural foods and have a large
    bulk section
Surplus and salvage chains
Costco
Local ethnic grocery stores
Local farmers' markets
Local food co-ops

Personal Care

I'm a big believer in the idea that looking your personal best can make you feel your best and be more confident, which helps in many facets of life. The months after the births of my children, when I let my grooming and exercise routine go to hell, were a dark, dark time in my life. I realized that there was no way I could reignite my business or even function normally without self-confidence. It became my mission to get the situation under control.

By focusing on getting healthy and spending time on beauty rituals, I pulled myself out of my funk. I started the process by giving myself pedicures. From there, I started exercising. After that, I got my diet under control. It was like a snowball effect, all stemming from the care of my toenails! A pedicure is not just a pedicure; it's one small way to love and appreciate yourself.

My love for all things girly and my personal vanity have

resulted in a lifelong quest to find and test the best products. I will be unloved by advertisers for saying this, but looking great is a process that requires time, discipline, and skill, *not* expensive brands. You can look fabulous using the drugstore brands.

Did you know that L'Oréal owns Lancôme, Redken, and several fancy European brands? And Estée Lauder owns Jane, a fabulous cheap drugstore brand of cosmetics? Other than one product, Prescriptives Camouflage Cream, I have yet to find one department store makeup brand that doesn't have a cheap drugstore equivalent. And honestly, the Prescriptives cream actually *is* cheap because it's highly concentrated. I use it every day to cover up my dark eye circles, and one tube lasts more than a year.

Like speaking French or staying on your diet while your friends are stuffing down crème brûlée, personal grooming is a skill—one that must be honed with dedication. Of course, we all know one or two annoyingly beautiful women who look perfect with no makeup, hair in a ponytail, and golden skin year-round. Naturally, these women are also perfectly toned and spend much of their time at the local yoga studio or meditating. For the rest of us mere mortals, looking good actually takes work. There are no shortcuts.

It really comes down to whether or not looking your best is a priority for you. Some women can't go to the grocery store without a full "face on," and others don't even own mascara. I'm all for whatever makes you feel happy. If doing your hair and makeup feels like a needless burden, then don't do it. But figuring out how to apply makeup and get your hair looking great all by yourself can be fun, and can even make you feel better. Tough financial times call for do-it-yourself resourcefulness. So find a girlfriend—you know, the capable one who always looks great—and have her over for some wine and a makeover. Or go get a makeover from a professional at your local mall and ask a lot of questions. Scour the library for back issues of beauty magazines for techniques. Then go home and practice.

In addition, daily exercise, healthy food, sunscreen, and smart grooming habits will leave you looking (and feeling) like a million bucks.

Frugal Beauty Hall of Fame

Dove soap (yes, even on acne)
Eucerin Extra Protective Moisture Lotion SPF 30, for the face
Maybelline Great Lash mascara
Wet n Wild eyeliner pencil
Maybelline blush
Cover Girl Outlast All-Day Lipcolor
Physicians Formula Powder Palette Multi-Colored Blush (as a bronzer)
Pantene Pro-V shampoo and conditioner[1]
Suave hair spray
Prescriptives Camouflage Cream
New York Color Smooth Skin Pressed Face Powder

Cars

Big car payments are one of the most efficient ways to keep you in a financial hole. Spending 50% of one's annual salary on a

---

1. Some drugstore shampoos and conditioners can, over time, weigh your hair down with a waxy coating, leaving it shiny but limp. Once a week, use a hard-core shampoo like Prell to strip off the buildup. Then you'll be good as new. Bumble and bumble has a fancy product for this purpose called Sunday Shampoo, but the cheap Prell does the same thing.

vehicle (as many people do) is absolutely insane. If you make $80,000 per year, you have no business owning a $40,000 car. This is lunacy. A more reasonable plan is to pay no more than 20% of your annual income on the combined costs of the vehicles in your household. That means that if your total household income is $100,000 and you own two cars, you should pay no more than $20,000 for those two cars *combined*. Spend as little as possible on a vehicle. A car is an expense—a depreciating asset—not an investment.

Lenders and auto dealerships will run a bunch of funny numbers and conveniently inform you what kind of monthly payment you can afford. I say *no* monthly payment is the best option. Don't be a debt slave. Pay cash and buy what you can afford. However, if you must have a car payment, aim for paying off the whole thing in two years.

Buying a New Car

There are many emotional factors involved with car buying, not just financial factors. Some people just have to buy new and would not consider a used vehicle. Much of the time, buying a new vehicle is financially irresponsible, but not always. The conditions necessary for a new car to make financial sense:

You plan to own it for more than ten years
You keep it spotless and maintain in perfectly
You buy it with cash

If you can meet these three criteria, here are some helpful tips for buying new. Also see Chapter 10, "Craigslist Is the New Black," and learn to negotiate in Chapter 11.

RULES FOR BUYING A NEW CAR

Rule 1: Haggle like your life depends on it (How to Talk a Dog Off a Meat Truck on page 164).

Rule 2: Run a search online to determine what the dealer's cost is, including any kickbacks the dealer is entitled to. Your offer should give the dealer a $200 to $500 net profit, no more.

Rule 3: Shop around. Check buying clubs like Costco to get additional discounts.

Rule 4: Aim for 20% off the sticker price.

Rule 5: Ignore confusing sales and rebates advertised in the paper or elsewhere. Focus on the price you're willing to pay.

Rule 6: Make the rounds to all the dealers and play them off each other.

Rule 7: Don't trade in. This does not make financial sense, period. Treat the sale of your existing car and your purchase of a car as two separate transactions. Sell your old car privately. Trading in makes you a sucker. The one exception to this rule is if the dealer will give you a much better trade-in value than you could get from a private-party sale (as sometimes occurs during specials or sales). Dealers aren't in the business of losing money or buying assets for more than they're worth (your car), so always be skeptical of this sort of deal.

Rule 8: The bottom line is the most important variable. What you spend is much more important than what you save.

Rule 9: Buy on the last day of the month, last day of the quarter, or last day of the year, because often the salesmen's bonuses are based on their performance during these periods, leaving them with incentive to knock prices down.

How to Drive for Free

The goal here is to sell your car for the same price you bought it for. I used a similar technique on two vehicles (my first two cars as a teenager). In my case, I actually sold the vehicles for *more* than I paid for them. I paid $1,500 for my 1985 Volkswagen Jetta and sold it for $1,800 two years later, resulting in a $300 profit. Same thing for my 1980 Volvo.

Step one: Buy a used car, either a repossessed one from your local commercial credit office, or from a private party. Choose an older model. In this example, you pay $4,000.

Step two: In about two years, when you get tired of that car, run an add to sell your "Classic 1990 Volvo" for $4,000 to a private party (never a dealership).

Step three: Buy another car as outlined in step one with the money from step two.

Step four: In another two years or so, run another "classic car" ad, and repeat.

The key for implementing this technique:

- Pick a brand that has a loyal following, and a reputation for making cars that last and hold value, e.g., Volvo, Subaru, VW, BMW, Toyota.

- Cherry-pick the car. Research used-car values ahead of

time, and spend your time looking for a vehicle that fits the above criteria and is underpriced at the dealership (or can be haggled down). You might have to visit ten places before you find a car that can be bought using this method.

- Pull out your money in $100 bills. Tell the dealer that you actually have an appointment to see another car, but if they'll sell you their car for X, you'll pay them with cash right now. (Your offer should be roughly half of what they are asking.)

- Expect that your offer will get rejected on occasion, and you might have to move on to the next seller.

BALLSY GIRL TRICK: PERFORM YOUR OWN CAR REPAIRS

The oxygen sensor light illuminated in my ten-year-old Mercedes literally one week before I was set to have an emissions test to get my license plates renewed. Of course the car didn't pass the emissions test, so I had to drive with expired plates until the car was repaired. A "car computer" repair sounded scary, technical, and expensive, so I glumly headed to the dealership to face my looming car repair bill. The dealership informed me that it would cost close to $1,000 to replace the little sensor. I informed them I would rather run outside and make snow angels in the nude than shell out that kind of dough for a tiny piece of plastic and wire. (That $1,000 could be much better spent getting my freckles lasered off.)

I returned home, defeated, but then I found an online community forum for Mercedes clunker owners. As it turns out, this repair was common for my model, and many of the forum users had fixed the problem themselves. The professional tightwads on the forum didn't even buy a new part, and they offered instructions on how to fix the old one. I ran out to my car, popped the hood open, yanked out the oxygen sensor, and immediately began to inspect the faulty part. After tinkering with it, I discovered that it was beyond repair. But I scored a new one on eBay for $100. It arrived in two days, it took me ten minutes to install, and voilà, that pesky oxygen sensor light went away.

Since then, I have performed three other do-it-yourself car repairs on my beloved clunker, saving myself thousands. The instructions are easy to find on the web or in a car repair manual (like the Chilton series). I prefer the online instructions because digital photo technology has enabled users to share step-by-step photos of the repair process, which makes things much easier.

But I should say, auto repair is not for everyone. You do it at your own risk, and I don't recommend that you attempt major repairs, like replacing a clutch or an entire transmission, unless you're a real auto mechanic. I'm simply suggesting that you get to know your car, and don't be intimidated by it.

Furniture

The online listings network craigslist is the ultimate furniture utopia. The convenience of armchair shopping, the variety and unbeatable prices of the items in its listings make craigslist my number-one venue for furniture shopping.

Most furniture is heavy and bulky, and therefore expensive to ship. For this reason, companies like IKEA have mastered the art of designing pieces that are light, come unassembled, and fit into tidy boxes. The problem with do-it-yourself assembly furniture is that it often falls apart after you move it once or twice. Set your sights on more substantial, solid pieces that will last for years to come.

The trick to buying furniture online is to know exactly what you're looking for. Otherwise, it can be an overwhelming experience.

I recently scored a solid walnut, classic mid-century modern American dresser on craigslist. The grainy photo in the ad revealed a pitiful sight. The poor thing had beautiful lines and solid, cast-brass hardware, but it had been shoved in someone's garage, complete with drippy paint stains and a dirty bicycle leaning on it. The owner was asking $35 and had to "get rid of it quick" because it was "taking up room in the garage." We rescued it the following day from its stinky garage prison, then sanded it, varnished it, gave it a big hug, and restored it to its former glory. The whole process involved two hours of work, if that. Now I get to enjoy this gleaming, gorgeous piece of furniture art every day.

Plus, as it turns out, this dresser was made by a famous Scandinavian artist hired in the 1950s by an American furniture manufacturer, and it's worth $3,000. Not that it matters, because I won't part with it.

Garage sales are another way to score great furniture. Of course, it takes consistent and repeated effort, because not every outing will result in finding a piece you love. But garage sale outings are fun and cheap entertainment for the whole family. The "treasure hunt" element adds extra drama to the experience.

The important thing to remember about furniture is that new does not mean better. In fact, old furniture is often much, much better because the construction and materials are superb. Look for pieces constructed of solid metal and solid wood, not particleboard or veneer over particleboard.

Remember that the design of old pieces can be gorgeous. If a piece has beautiful lines, thoughtful detail, or hand-sculpted elements, try to ignore the ugly finish or color. A fresh coat of paint or varnish can transform any well-made, solid-wood piece. Get thee to the library and check out *Better Homes & Gardens* back issues or books that specialize in the trash-to-treasure concept.

And don't feel guilty when you lovingly restore or revitalize a piece of furniture that turns out to be highly valuable. It's not your problem that its former owner didn't appreciate the piece. You've rescued, recycled, and cared for something that somebody else wanted to dump. Keep it and enjoy it.

UPHOLSTERY: IF IT STINKS, REDO IT

When buying upholstered pieces, recognize that upholstery is made of fiber, which absorbs odors, dust mites, pet dander, and anything else that touches it. When you get it home, you might discover an unpleasant odor or general ickiness and decide to reupholster it. Reupholstering old furniture is not as scary as it sounds. Anyone with an electric staple gun, patience, and a piece of fabric can do it. Check out your local library for books on upholstery. Then dive in.

Reupholstering is also a great opportunity to make a piece of furniture more livable. I recently replaced some very fancy (but nasty) upholstery on some old dining chairs with washable zippered cushions. If you have children, you might consider making slipcovers or even zippered cushions that you can throw in the wash when they get dirty from Popsicles and grimy little fingers.

Reupholstering need not be an expensive process. First of all, if the foam in an old piece of furniture is still good, keep it, because the foam can be very costly. You can throw it in a bathtub with bleach and water to kill any dust mites, mold, fungus, or whatever other mysteries in there might be close to discovering fire and the wheel. Bleach is great at getting rid of the ickiness completely. Then, simply rinse the foam out and let it dry in the sun. Once you have clean foam, you can go from there and shop for deals on fabric.

Clothes

Recent economic studies have shown that the retail prices of women's clothes have not gone up with inflation as much as other consumables, like food. This is a great thing. Let's hope that trend continues. If it doesn't, it might be time to come up with a wardrobe strategy.

Even with escalating shipping costs and inflation, the big warehouse stores like Costco and surplus retailers like T.J. Maxx will still be offering great deals on clothes, relative to other retailers. I am astounded at the deals that can be found at T.J. Maxx in particular. Cute pants for $10? High-quality Ralph Lauren T-shirts for $12? I've paid more than that to park downtown for ten minutes. If these stores can continue to offer these prices over the next several years, then their business is going to do very well. I, for one, will continue to shop there.

If retail shops do end up really jacking up their prices because of inflation and other factors, thrift shopping for clothes will be a great option. Thrift shopping is great for specialty clothing, including maternity wear and bridal wear. You can save yourself loads of money. Think about it: you wear maternity clothes for only a few months, and then you'll want to burn them. Don't succumb to the temptation to waste money on new maternity wear if you can find a lot in your size on craigslist, or even borrow some from a friend. The same goes for bridal. Seriously, why would you drop several thousand bucks on a dress you will (hopefully!) only wear once? Think spending an extra $3,000 on your dress is going to make you look any more gorgeous than you already are? It's not. It's the woman who makes the dress look beautiful, not the other way around. And trust me, you can find tons of great wedding dresses for a song if you shop smart.

RECESSION HEAT INDEX			
	SMOKIN' HOT	TEPID	CHILLED
Food prep	Mega-cooking	Making dinner at home	Takeout
Forehead fixer	Bangs	Botox	Forehead lift
Vodka	Cheap brand run through a Brita	High-end brand	Celebrity-endorsed brand
Shopping online	Negotiation	Sniping	Comparing
Fitness	Jumping rope in your kitchen	Gym membership	Personal trainers
Hair color	At-home highlights	Going brunette	$200 salon highlights
Car payment	Paying cash for a three-year-old car	Five-year financing	Leasing

10

Craigslist Is the New Black

The Neighborhood Garage Sale Has Gone High Tech

Are you a thrift shopping novice? Would you rather run naked around your neighborhood than get caught purchasing a secondhand coat? News flash: paying retail is so yesterday. Thrift shopping is the future, whether at a traditional thrift store or through an online venue like eBay or craigslist. Your thrifting skills will not just come in handy—they will likely become essential during an economic downturn.

Thrift shopping is like a push-up bra: sometimes thrilling, sometimes disheartening, but always there when you need a pick-me-up. Of course, buying everything used is probably an unrealistic goal, but you can save a whole lot of dough by thinking twice before paying retail. Here is a short list of things that are great to purchase used.

Cars
Clothing
Sports equipment
Kitchen and household goods
Books, CDs, and DVDs
Electronics and appliances
Computers
Tools
Toys and kid's stuff

If all of this is new to you, fear not. Once you immerse yourself in thrifty nirvana, you will come to embrace it whole-heartedly. Secondhand shopping is like any skill; it takes time, effort, and persistence. But once you get the hang of it, hell, you'll probably come to love it.

The prices of new retail consumer goods and products are going through the roof. So get ready, ladies. Out-of-control inflation, high transportation costs, and our displacement of locally produced goods is going to cost us big dollars at the cash register. For example, those who covet $200 designer denim from brands like 7 for All Mankind or Rock & Republic had better hold on to their rivets. Those jeans could be headed into the $400 to $500 range.

But not only high-end goods will be affected. The cheaper versions may see even bigger price bumps. Buying used is a smart and practical way to avoid depressingly high price tags at the mall.

An added benefit of buying used goods is that it's a much more environmentally friendly way to shop. No huge plastic packaging to dispose of, no heavy-duty cardboard boxes swathed in layer upon layer of petroleum plastic, and no wasting of fossil fuel during its long haul from China. Shipping costs increased from $3,000 per container in 2001 to $8,000 in

2008, and they're expected to go up to $15,000 per container when oil hits $200 a barrel. All those transportation costs will translate to significantly higher purchase prices for new items. Now that we're familiar with the "why" of thrifting, let's get down to the business of "how," shall we?

BRICK-AND-MORTAR THRIFT SHOPS

As shoppers across the U.S. have tightened their belts, thrift shops have seen a big upswing in business since the beginning of 2008. *The New York Times* reported in June 2008 that even the Madison Avenue crowd, which normally shops for brand new Jimmy Choo shoes and Chloé bags, is suddenly hunting the local high-end thrift shops for slightly used versions. Pride keeps them from disclosing the real reason (wallet tightening), so they insist that they're trying to recycle and be "more environmentally conscious." But we all know the real reason. And it's okay—everybody is thrift shopping. From Wall Street to the country girls, nobody's immune to the recession. Suddenly, it's chic to buy used clothes.

The other side of thrift is selling the things you no longer need to consignment shops. You're not going to get back 100% of what you paid for that handbag (usually), but you might get 30%, and that can add up to some decent pocket change. You might consider rifling through your closets and trying to sell through consignment things you no longer use. You can get some extra cash, or a credit at your local consignment shop.

ONLINE THRIFTINESS

When thinking of online thrift shopping, two names immediately come to mind: craigslist and eBay. The former (www .craigslist.org) is like a virtual garage sale and community gathering place for practically everything from clothing to Yanni concert tickets. You don't pay shipping because the final transactions usually take place face-to-face. You're dealing with someone who lives near you, not an anonymous seller sporting a name like CherryPuss2006 or Liv4RoCK-Nyou. Craigslist is also a phenomenal way to sell goods that you no longer need, like that plastic baby swing that's been parked in the corner of your garage for the last eight years. Particularly fantastic is the fact that craigslist does not charge any listing fees (thanks to founder Craig Newmark). It's free to both buyers and sellers.

Craigslist can save you loads of money, provide cheap access to many of your basic consumer goods, and deliciously supply the primordial urge to hunt.[1] The best part of craigslist, and the most addictive, is the occasional jaw-dropping surprise item. Try going back to IKEA after you've stumbled upon a mint-condition mid-century Danish Modern teak armchair that's been hiding out at Granny's house since 1945, selling for fifteen bucks. That's almost a dirty thrill. The retail stores simply cannot compete with that sort of euphoria.

For those of you living under a rock, www.ebay.com is the 800-pound gorilla of the online auction market. It has fundamentally changed the way people shop. It has turned every Tom, Dick, and Sally with a pile of junk in the basement into an instant entrepreneur with their own virtual store.

If you're looking for something in particular (say, a 1970s Victorian Revival wedding dress studded with faux pearls and iridescent sequins), then look no further than eBay. Type in your description and eBay will spit out several, if not several

---

1. Warning: Repetitive daily scouring of craigslist can become an addiction and may indeed require a 12-step program to remove you from its clutches.

hundred, items that fit your bill. Now brace yourself for the combat—I mean bidding, which can be unpleasant if not downright vicious.

Disciplined and sophisticated eBayers with a bone to pick and too much free time have cleverly honed a skill known as "sniping." In other words, they hover over an auction, waiting patiently until the last possible moment, at which time they dive in for the kill and outbid you a second before the auction closes. It's a dog-eat-dog world. Be prepared to fight dirty if you want to win the eBay game.

If you do happen to lose some lovely trinket on eBay to a sniper, take solace in the knowledge that future eBay listings will hold even lovelier trinkets to come, and you might score an even better deal than the one you lost. At least that is what you must remind yourself of at 4:00 in the morning as you find yourself clenching your fists and shouting at your computer as the clock ticks down and the price of your "find" shoots to the moon. Do not, under any circumstances, get caught in the sniper's trap of increasing your bid again and again. It's cruel but true—some snipers actually view this as a form of entertainment. Know your maximum bid beforehand and stick to it.

A point worth mentioning is that the shipping fees on eBay will be increasing as oil costs rise. So that cute widget that costs you $5 might cost you $10 to ship. In some cases, the deal is still worth it, but in most cases the cost of shipping will suddenly place that widget in the range between Expensive and Are You Kidding Me? Shopping locally, however, eliminates shipping costs altogether, which is particularly important for bulky, heavy items like furniture.

11

Four Skills You Need

Four Essential Recession Skills

I. LEARN A NEW LANGUAGE

As the dollar free-falls, the financial opportunities abroad will be plentiful. When the U.S. dollar drops, prices for U.S. goods get cheaper for buyers overseas. Do you know that it costs roughly $50 U.S. for two coffees and a tart in France? In comparison, the same purchase at Panera Bread in suburban America might cost $6.50. Things are cheaper in the U.S., including white-collar service employees (such as computer programmers, customer service reps, etc.). What this means, ultimately, is that job opportunities and business opportunities await us overseas.

To take full advantage of these opportunities, you should speak at least one language besides English. For my business, I tried for years communicating in English to Chinese suppliers, with horrible results. Eventually, I had to buckle down and teach myself Mandarin (the official language of China).

Which Languages?

According to www.gov, these are the most commonly spoken languages in the world and the total number of people who speak the language, including those who speak it as their second language.

Mandarin, 1.051 billion
English, 508 million
Hindi/Urdu, 466 million
Arabic (all varieties), 452 million
Spanish, 382 million
Russian, 255 million
Bengali, 211 million
Portuguese, 192 million
Indonesian, 163 million
German, 123 million
Japanese, 123 million
French, 115 million

There is no reliable way to verify these numbers, mostly because there are no reliable census data for certain languages. But you get the big picture.

When examining the global economy, job opportunities, and business opportunities, Mandarin, Hindi/Urdu, Spanish, Portuguese, Russian, and Arabic would all be useful to you. Sorry, French . . . as sexy as you are, you won't pay the bills.

My number one pick is Mandarin. China will continue to grow economically, even as the U.S. plunges into a deep, prolonged recession. It is considered by many well-known economists to be *the* world economic superpower. There are many opportunities for Westerners who can speak Mandarin well.

Also, the much ignored and overlooked Brazil is an up-

and-coming powerhouse because it has become the world's biggest exporter of raw materials. Brazilians are getting rich at an alarming rate. Portuguese would be my number two pick.

My number three pick is Russian. Suddenly, Russia has moved from has-been to front-rank. Russia is the world's second leading producer of oil, after Saudi Arabia. It is not dependent on other nations for its energy needs. In fact, Russia consumes less energy than it produces and is becoming stronger and more prosperous.

Arabic comes in at number four on my language learning list. As long as we are dependent upon the Middle East for oil there will be opportunities for Arabic speakers.

Hooked on China

In the next decade, Mandarin will become the new "must-learn" language. Panama recently implemented a bold change in its school system by making classes in Mandarin a requirement for all schoolchildren. So now the little kids of Panama will be learning Mandarin, not English. I suspect that many other countries will be following suit. In the U.S., the number of schools offering Mandarin as part of the curriculum is steadily increasing. If you want to know more about the many opportunities in China, I suggest financial expert Jim Rogers's fabulous book *A Bull in China: Investing Profitably in the World's Greatest Market.*

Since we're on the topic of kids, consider learning a language with them. My little ones are learning Mandarin, and hearing them speak it (and sing Chinese songs) is amazingly cute. Also, I have found that it's great fun publicly reprimanding them in Mandarin. Everything sounds so much cooler in Mandarin, especially, "Let go of your sister's hair or I will revoke your *Sesame Street* privileges for three months."

Conquering the Self-Doubt of Language Learning

If you're the way I used to be, you might resist trying to learn a foreign language because of self-doubt and thoughts such as . . .

How will I find the time? It takes only thirty minutes per day to become fluent in any language. And these thirty minutes can occur while you are showering, doing the dishes, or giving yourself a mani/pedi.

My school days are over. I can't sit in a classroom, and homework sounds dreadful. You don't need to take classes. You can learn right at home with an audio language program.

It sounds too hard. Boredom makes things seem difficult. Finding a fun and engaging way to learn will make it easy.

I don't have an "aptitude" for languages. I love this excuse because it's totally ridiculous. We all have an aptitude for languages. It is a part of your brain. If you can read this, then somewhere along the way, you learned English, which means you can learn other languages. I too was brainwashed by teachers who convinced me that languages were "just not my thing." My newly acquired "native" Chinese accent begs to differ.

How to Learn Any Language in Three Months

My Mandarin dreams were fulfilled the day I discovered the key to mastering any language: the Pimsleur Approach language program.[1] Pimsleur Approach is divided into thirty-

---

1. There are other good language programs out there, like Rosetta Stone and Berlitz. Pimsleur Approach is the one I use. (Pimsleur is not sponsoring me or paying me to say this.)

minute audio lessons. No textbooks, no tedious drills, no homework, no written exercises. This meant I could learn Chinese while driving my little ones to preschool, doing the dishes, or exercising.

I loaded the whole Pimsleur Mandarin series onto my iPod and started a daily ritual of doing the lessons while walking around my neighborhood at a frantic pace. My neighbors now think I'm crazy. There she goes, the strange white girl talking to herself in Chinese. What makes it even funnier is that many of my neighbors happen to be Chinese.

I am a woman on a mission. I will be fluent in Mandarin. Nothing can deter me from my ritual. When the stormy Seattle sky looms large and gray, I put on my rain gear and head out for Chinese time. Recently, five minutes into my walk, the sky dropped buckets of hail down on me, at which point I found shelter under a large maple tree, shrieking, "Wo hen hao!" ("I'm doing very well!") to anyone who cared to listen.

Does this sound too good to be true? I thought so. Just to make sure the Pimsleur lessons were working, I started gabbing regularly with my Mandarin-speaking friends and acquaintances. They were surprised to hear that I was learning Mandarin, and completely shocked when they heard my "authentic" Beijing accent. (Pimsleur teaches formal-sounding Mandarin with a Beijing accent.) One friend is convinced that I must have been Chinese in a former life.

When I have questions about words and phrases not covered in the Pimsleur series ("I need mint chocolate chip ice cream right now"), I consult my favorite online Chinese English Dictionary, at www.mdbg.net. In addition to the clear and concise pronunciations, the website provides the "pinyin" version, phonetically spelling out the words using our alphabet.

Racking up fifteen to twenty miles of speed-walking per week during Chinese time has resulted in more than just great Pu tong hua (which means "Mandarin," or "the People's language"). I've lost several pounds in the process, my skin has improved, and the daily dose of fresh air feels great.

2. Be Able to Fix Things

Ask yourself: Do I have any practical skills that could either generate income or be traded to get something I need? The massive DIY (do-it-yourself) industry is going to pay off big time for people who have been living it and learning from it. People who have cultivated everyday practical skills—carpenters, cooks, seamstresses, electricians, handymen/women—will be in demand. Learn how to fix a toilet, solder metal components, splice electrical wire, or change a headlight on your car. You can find books and DVDs at your local library as well as detailed videos on YouTube on how to do all sorts of stuff.

If you don't possess any trade skills, it is very important to be willing to learn them now or down the road. Are you among the many who think plunging a toilet is beneath you? If so, this recession could eat you alive. Willingness to try to learn new things, particularly skills that make you more self-reliant, is a key personality indicator that will separate the sinkers from the swimmers.

Your expertise in workstation management systems analysis will not help if your roof springs a leak and there's no extra money to hire a contractor to fix the problem. Figure it out yourself—you can do it!

3. Learn to Negotiate

How to Talk a Dog off a Meat Truck

Perhaps the most valuable skill in dubious economic times is the skill of negotiation. Everything is negotiable, whether in your personal life (the price of a car or how often your man does the vacuuming), or in business (rent, cost of advertising or supplies). This is true during a good economy and even more so during a weak economy. Hard times call for the ability to cut the best deal, negotiate like your Jewish grandmother, and sometimes get even more than you deserve.

Most Americans consider haggling uncomfortable, awkward, and unnecessary. Honing your skills in the bargaining department can help you financially in ways you can't even imagine. Growing up, I watched in awe (and sometimes embarrassment) as my mother utilized her wits and haggling skills to get us hotel rooms at Disney World, tickets to events, and other stuff that we would not otherwise have been able to afford.

Many of her skills seeped into my psyche (or it's in our gene pool, who knows), and I've used it to my advantage countless times. Like the time that I tearfully negotiated with the TA over my final grade in fluid dynamics. I really needed a B in that class, not an F; I was just about to graduate with my engineering degree, and it was do or die. He asked me to do a few problems on the spot to prove I knew the subject matter. I completed the problems, sobbing the whole time. After using up his box of Kleenex, I got my B and left smiling. I think he was relieved just to get me the hell out of his office, honestly. (See rules 3 and 5 in Rules of Bargaining, below).

Channeling the Indian Art of Negotiation

I got great lessons in negotiation on a trip to India, where haggling is right up there with loving your mother and breathing. Everybody does it, and every single transaction in India is negotiated. Even when you're buying a piece of celery, you haggle. I can tell you firsthand from dealing with the jewelry dealers in Mumbai, it's an understatement to say that Indians are shrewd negotiators. It's a fact and a way of life there. And boy, they can teach us a thing or two.

The founder of Hotmail, Sabeer Bhatia, learned negotiation strategy as a child, watching his family's servants haggling over groceries in Bangalore. His negotiation prowess came in very handy as an adult dealing with Bill Gates. Sabeer successfully pushed Microsoft into upping the acquisition price of Hotmail from $200 million to $400 million.

RULES OF BARGAINING

Rule 1: The "true" price of anything is what someone is willing to pay for it *right then*. Retail prices are nothing but numbers on a piece of paper. This goes for houses especially, by the way.

Rule 2: Meet in the middle. Set your first offer with the following formula:

Your first offer = 50% to 75% of your goal price

If the retail price is $1,000 (their first offer), and you want to pay $750 (your goal price), then your first offer should be around $500.

$$500 = 67\% \text{ of } \$750$$

The other side might come back with $850. Then you'll offer to "compromise" at $650. And then you can jointly agree on "splitting the difference" at $750. Meeting them halfway at this point makes the seller feel that you're accommodating them, although you planned it all along.

Rule 3: Make the seller show you lots of items. Be quiet and let them expend loads of energy taking you around, blabbing on and on about the variety of merchandise from which you can select. The goal is to use up their time and physical and mental energy. You need to get the seller invested in the transaction.

Rule 4: If you're going to buy more than one item, do not let on that you plan to do so. Act like you're going to buy only one item, and negotiate each item separately. Once the price of each item has been cut by 50%, or whatever, ask the seller if he could give you a better deal if you bought both items. You might be able to get an additional 5% to 10% off this way. Then ask what he can do for you if you add a third item (probably another 5%). Now surprise the seller by showing interest in a fourth item that is much more expensive than the others. You don't actually have to intend to buy the fourth item, but have the seller run the numbers anyway. At this point, he might reduce the prices of the first three items. Secure the prices of the first three items and don't buy the expensive item.

Rule 5: Use charm. You know, that skill you honed at age four to get Mom to buy you an ice cream cone? Employ subtle tactics, such as a slight tilt of the head, a smile, or sweet tone in your voice. Humor is also charming and very effective. Do it. It works. Always try charm first, and resort to crying if the situation demands it. Most guys don't like it when women cry. If you're dealing with a guy, you might be able to get your way with tears. He'll either feel sorry for you or, more likely, just want you to leave. Either way, you win.

Rule 6: Shush! Recoil in silence and shock after the sellers offer their first discount price. Don't be afraid of silence. It can be a vital part of negotiations. Staring in silence for a long time often results in the sellers offering to reduce the price. This can be tricky for Americans not accustomed to bargaining. The sudden adrenaline rush and nerves might cause you to spoil the deal by turning on your blabbermouth. If nerves get to you, try quietly tapping your foot instead.

Rule 7: Be prepared to walk out if you must. You have to have a walk-away price fixed in your head. Decide the absolute maximum you will pay, and walk away if you don't get it. If the seller has already invested a lot of time and energy in you, it's doubtful he'll let you leave before he lowers the price further.

Rule 8: Pretend you're not the decision maker. Having an imaginary "boss" with veto power will allow you to drive a hard bargain and make ridiculous demands without seeming like a complete asshole. Your real or fictional husband can play the boss role perfectly. This technique will remove any hostility from the negotiating environment. And you might even get some pity points from your opponent from being married to such an oppressive bastard.

Rule 9: Some people just won't play ball or don't have the authority to haggle with you. If this happens to you, go for a walk and come back later when another person is on duty.

How to Negotiate a Hotel Room at the Last Minute

You arrive at your destination with only $125 to spend on a room, but you know that this hotel typically averages $300 a night.

Desk Clerk: "Good afternoon. How can I help you today?"

You: "Hi, how are you? I'm so glad to be here finally, the weather is so amazing. Hey listen, I have two little kids that suck every ounce of energy and money out of me, so we're on a budget. Anything you can do for me would be fantastic, like AAA, or a discount for geezers or something like that. I would really appreciate it." (Strategy A, below.)

Desk Clerk: "Well . . . we are booked, but I can probably squeak you in a room. How does $150 sound?"

You: [*Stare silently for a few moments.*] (Strategy B) "Hmmm . . . well, that might be more than we can afford. Let me check with my husband. [*You pick up the phone and talk to your real or fictitious husband briefly.*] Darn, we can't spend that much. Is there a room for about $100? Do you have anything at all, like even a really small room with a view of the Dumpster?" (Strategy C)

Desk Clerk: "Let me check with my manager. [Desk clerk leaves, then returns a few minutes later.] We can get you in a room for $125."

You: "Fantastic! Thank you so much. I really appreciate it."

Notice how at first, you're not placing any demands, and not even really asking for anything. All you're doing here is being friendly and interjecting some humor into the life of someone who might otherwise have a very dull day (the desk clerk).

NEGOTIATING STRATEGIES

A. Here you use the silence trick. Silence is most effectively used after their first offer.

B. You're pretending your husband is the boss and decision
    maker, entitling you to continue haggling with the desk
    clerk without seeming like a complete douche bag.

C. Humor is a great way to establish camaraderie.

How to Negotiate Lower Tuition

You really want little Johnny to take classes in piano/Spanish/
Montessori/basketball/ballet/acrobatics/sculpting/whatever.
But you're trying to save money and these classes are breaking
the budget. And if he doesn't stay busy, he'll be blowing up
homemade volcanoes, spewing ketchup into every crevice of
your kitchen, then posting it on YouTube. Classes are a must.

> You (on the phone): "Hi, I'm really hoping you
> have some space left in your Spanish for Little
> Gringos class. Please say you do."
>
> School: "No. I'm sorry, we're completely booked."
>
> You: Oh, heck. Johnny's dream will be crushed. He
> worships Dora, Diego, and J. Lo. Are you sure
> you don't have any room at all? Not even a lit-
> tle spot in the corner? My son is really polite.
> You won't even notice he's there. He could
> help you clean up after class if you are inter-
> ested in a work trade." (Strategy D, below)
>
> School: "Well, I could use some help getting the room
> ready for the next class."
>
> You: "Great! How long would it take?"
>
> School: "Maybe about ten to fifteen minutes. If he
> wants to do a work trade, we can offer you a
> reduced tuition of, say, $50."

You: "That sounds perfect. See you next week."

NEGOTIATING STRATEGY

D. Imply that you or your husband could offer some service.
    For example, offer to come in once a month to teach
    a special seminar on something (art, music, a foreign
    culture, slam-dunking technique, etc.). If you have any
    graphic arts skills, offer to help the school with website
    design or posters. If the school has an auction or fund-
    raising event, that's another way to volunteer.

4. CULTIVATE A STRONG MIND

PERSPECTIVE CHECK FROM THE GREAT DEPRESSION

"I was glad I was brought up in those times, as you really
learn to appreciate and take care of things."

—*Alma Smith, Woodville, Wisconsin.*

From *Stories and Recipes of the Great Depression of the 1930's* by
Rita Van Amber (see Resources.)

Attitude is everything in life. Your attitude is the only thing
that you truly have any control over. You cannot completely
control the events in your life, how other people react, or what

they might think or do to you. But you can control your attitude toward those events or people.

As an entrepreneur, I have had far more failures than
successes. I view failure as a learning tool. People tend to
take success for granted, but they often feel and remember
every failure. Every time I have a failure or setback, I look
at it as an opportunity to learn, and trust that I was meant
to have the experience to propel me forward. Rolling with
the punches that life throws at me has somewhat delayed my
long journey toward my goals, but it has made me adjust my
path along the way.

I look at the current recession as the biggest opportunity
of my lifetime. There will be tremendous change and tremendous opportunity as the massive credit bubble unwinds. It will
remove the plague of materialism that seems to affect every
facet of American culture, and it will force people to become
acquainted again with their families and neighbors. For those
who are financially prepared, it will present fantastic opportunities to acquire assets for pennies on the dollar. For those
who are struggling financially, it will provide an opportunity
for resourcefulness and self-reliance, and the confidence building that comes with those actions. The recession will clean out
all the excesses that have been built into our society over the
last twenty years. It will put in place a much stronger founda-
tion for America to build upon and contribute to the global
economy.

You will need flexibility and a positive attitude to thrive
in the coming years. Remember what your parents told you
when you were growing up: You can do anything you set your
mind to. The Internet has made it so much easier. You can
now go online and Google can help you fix or make almost
anything, complete with videos, technical diagrams, detailed
instructions, and step-by-step pictures. You can find contract

manufacturers for business, customers, food recipes, and how-to instructions on almost any topic. I read a story about a high school science student who researched on the web how to make an actual nuclear bomb minus the plutonium. Everything is available now, and unlimited opportunities are only a mouse click or phone call away. You just need a willingness to try, a positive attitude, and an understanding that it's okay to make mistakes.

Generalization versus Specialization

In the last thirty years we have seen the rise of the expert. People now know much more about very narrowly focused fields. Globalization and technology contributed heavily to this trend. I believe the coming recession will reverse this as economics once again become more localized and communities more self-reliant. There will always be a need for experts, but I believe their recent dominance will subside.

A positive attitude toward learning, optimism, and the ability to solve a wide range of problems will be invaluable skills in the next decade. It always amazes me how people think they need to be trained in something before they'll try it. Just do it. Think of Georgia O'Keeffe, who dropped out of art school when she discovered she could teach herself better than anyone else could. Doing is the best teacher.

Adaptability to Change

There is potential for some dramatic changes to happen in the near future. Your ability to adapt will help determine your success. What if the U.S. experiences a complete currency collapse, as happened to Weimar Germany in the late 1920s, and to post–Soviet Russia, and, seven years ago, Argentina? What will you do if all of a sudden your bank goes bankrupt and you lose all your savings because the FDIC does not have the funds to pay for the "guaranteed" coverage? The FDIC can currently cover only 1.22% of insured deposits. One big bank wipeout and the FDIC is bankrupt. These things are not likely to happen, but they could. Your ability to adapt to change is vital.

A very realistic possibility is $20 per gallon for gas. This may sound crazy, but let's look back ten years. In 1998, gas was around $1.20 per gallon. At the time I wrote this book, it was $4.50, though it has been in the $3.30 to $4.00 range at times. That's almost a sixfold increase in the price of gas. I know, technically $4.50 is less than four times $1.20, but let's look at the number more closely. The federal and state gas taxes take up about 50 cents a gallon. Gas minus taxes in 1998 was about 70 cents, and today it's about $4, which is almost a 600% increase. If we get another 600% increase, that will put gas at $24.50 per gallon. In the United Kingdom it is already $15 USD per gallon. For those of you who commute 30 miles each way to work, how will this affect you? Let's assume optimistically your car gets 30 mpg and gas is $20 per gallon. You'll use two gallons a day commuting. That works out to $200 a week just to get to work. And that doesn't even count taking little Spencer to soccer and music lessons. In the Midwest, families are now spending up to 15% of their annual incomes on gasoline.

I have a favorite movie scene from the animated film *Antz*. The ants are marching along single file, and a twig falls across the line and disrupts their path. The ants begin to panic, not knowing what to do, until their leader shows them that they can walk around the twig. Unfortunately, many people in our society have stopped thinking for themselves and just want to be told what to do. They still have the ability to solve problems, but it hasn't been used for a long time and many are afraid to use it again. According to bookstatistics.com, 42% of college graduates never read another book after graduation, and 80% of U.S. households did not buy a book last year. Life will become even more challenging for those unwilling to learn and think for themselves, so it's important that you become aware of the possibilities and that you walk into the next decade with your eyes and ears open. The dinosaurs didn't adapt to change very well, and we all know what happened to them.

LEAVING YOUR EGO AT THE DOOR

The ego is a double-edged sword. It's a vital component of our being and a driving force behind many who achieve tremendous financial success. However, it can also be a destructive force that causes us to make irrational decisions and take excessive risks. In the next decade, humility and generosity will be invaluable. The days of competing over who has the biggest diamond ring, the fanciest Lexus, the most vacation homes, etc., are coming to an end. We're already seeing a big shift in attitudes about material possessions. The driver of the big Hummer now garners scornful glances rather than admiration.

If your self-worth is wrapped up in what you own versus who you are, you need to shift your paradigm very quickly. That is your ego talking. A recent story in *The New York Times* talked about an investment banker whose income has dropped from $8 million per year to $2 million (I know, what a tough life!). Well, this banker wouldn't tell his wife his income has dropped because he was afraid she would divorce him. Instead, he borrowed millions so she could still take extravagant vacations and spend the way she was accustomed to spending. It all ended very badly for both of them. Because their egos could not accept reality, they chose to put themselves on an unsustainable path toward self-destruction. It doesn't matter if your income is $2 million a year or $20,000. You need to be aware and honest about your situation, tell your ego to go to hell, and make the right decisions to protect you and your family. Who cares what the neighbors think? If they're so wrapped up in what you have, they're not friends worth having anyway. You can't control what they think (and it's not worth trying, anyway), but you can control what you think.

12

Self-Sufficiency

Teaching Your Kids to Change Their Own Diapers and Other Useful Tricks

Many levels of self-sufficiency will come in handy during this recession. To be self-sufficient you don't need to start spinning your own wool for clothes or tapping the maple trees in your backyard for syrup. Whether you grow your own herbs on a windowsill or use solar panels to supplement your energy needs, taking even small steps toward self-reliance is both environmentally sound and budget friendly.

GROWING YOUR OWN FOOD

Mini-farming, urban farming, permaculture, square foot gardening, bio-intensive farming, and many other methods of growing food have begun to hit the mainstream. No longer the domain of hippies, environmental activists, and half-naked PETA protestors, growing your own food is suddenly chic.

PERSPECTIVE CHECK FROM
THE GREAT DEPRESSION

ℰℓℊ

"We were more fortunate to live on a farm than in a town or city. The chief priority on the farm was to feed the animals and ourselves. . . . As tough as it was, there was peace and happiness and a family love and respect that is nearly gone these days. We learned how to work."

—*Betty Ewers, Holcombe, Wisconsin.*

From *Stories and Recipes of the Great Depression of the 1930's* by Rita Van Amber (see Resources).

Consider that to feed one person using traditional agriculture methods takes $\frac{1}{3}$ to $\frac{3}{4}$ acre of land. Using bio-intensive farming methods, you can grow enough food to continuously feed one person a purely vegetarian, chemical-free diet on less than $\frac{1}{10}$ acre.[1]

If you have access to a lawn, patio, deck, or roof, you can grow your own food—delicious, nutritious, pesticide-free, fresh food. You can even borrow lawn space from a neighbor or find rental land on craigslist.

If you think growing your own food will require lots of time hoeing and weeding, drudgery, and general slavery, think again. New mini-farming methods feature:

---

1. Amy Stewart, "The Man Who Would Feed the World." www.sfgate.com, April 13, 2002.

Raised beds, completely aboveground
Very little if any weeding
No digging, heavy lifting, or grunt work
Much less effort than traditional garden methods
Five times as much food produced in the same space
No tilling
Using very few seeds, with none going to waste
Very low water requirements
Low space requirements
No fertilizers or chemicals of any kind
Cheap tools—only a small trowel, a pencil, and a pair of scissors are required
No gasoline-powered equipment of any kind
Very little time spent maintaining
Huge harvests in a tiny space
The ability to be set up anywhere, even a concrete patio, staircase, or deck railing
Use of recycled coffee, eggshells, and produce scraps to make compost and boost output

There are many sources of information on growing your own food. However, if you want a method that requires hardly any work or time and produces huge harvests, try Mel Bartholomew's *All New Square Foot Gardening*. Mel, who is on a mission to end world hunger, has traveled the globe teaching his methods. He has helped millions of people reclaim their dignity, giving them the tools to sustain themselves and nutritiously feed themselves and their families.

You and your family can use this method easily too. In fact, with the sudden escalation in food prices, you can turn your front yard into a moneymaking machine. You can sell your harvests to local restaurants, organic markets, your neighbors, or farmers' markets. With bell peppers going for $3.00 each, you can make a tidy profit on these alone.

A tiny 4' x 4' raised garden bed with good sun exposure can produce the following vegetables in one growing season.

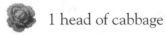 1 head of cabbage

1 head of broccoli

1 head of cauliflower

4 heads of romaine lettuce

4 heads of red lettuce

4 heads of leaf lettuce, then 16 scallions

4 heads of salad lettuce

4 pounds of sugar peas

8 bunches of Swiss chard

9 bunches of spinach, then 9 turnips

16 small ball carrots

16 beets, plus 4 bunches beet greens

16 long carrots

32 radishes

Source: Mel Bartholomew, *All New Square Foot Gardening*
(Cool Springs Press, 2006)

A family of four can get the majority of its calories and nutrition from less than 200 square feet of raised-bed garden space. Even if your goal is not to raise all of your own produce, consider a small garden bed.

GETTING YOUR KIDS TO HELP

Give a man a fish, and he'll eat today.
Teach a man to fish, and he'll eat for a lifetime.

—*Chinese proverb*

If you have children, they should be contributing to the workload of the family in some way. The last thing you want is to raise a bunch of lazy freeloaders who can't even take care of themselves, much less your future grandchildren. And if this happens, you have nobody to blame but yourself (and, perhaps, your husband's gene pool). Let's not turn your little darlings into another generational cliché. Instead, give them the tools to do good things for themselves and others.

An economic shitstorm is the perfect timing for implementing a team-oriented approach to the family's workload. I'm not talking about yanking your kids out of school so they can work a job (which is exactly what happened during the Great Depression, by the way). I'm talking about delegating basic household tasks fairly among everyone. This will free up your time so that you can start a business, work on an income backup plan, or kick your feet up and have a glass of wine.

Ironically, working mothers are often the ones who pick up the slack around the house, when in fact they need the most help. If you are a working mother, ask yourself: Do you end up doing most of the housework, even after a long day at work? Do you feel guilty making your children work around the house? Do you feel too stressed out to teach your children how to care for your home?

News flash: overcoddled children can't do for themselves. By "protecting" your children from housework, you are actually doing the opposite. By not allowing them opportunities to accomplish jobs and reap the rewards of a job well done, you prevent them from learning the skills necessary to lead an independent, free life. If you don't teach them, who will?

THE WORKING FAMILY

If you have children, rather than looking at yourselves as working parents, I encourage you to think of your family as a "working family." This sends the message that everyone, including the children, is a citizen of the household. Everyone who lives there contributes in some way. The benefit of this system is that the children will feel they're contributing members of the household, and that importance will give them a boost in self-esteem and self-worth.

Hard economic times force a certain degree of camaraderie among families, neighbors, friends, and communities. Cooperating families have the lifelong benefit of the closeness that develops from the healthy dependency and cooperation they share.

You will be surprised at how much a child can, and will, eagerly do. Even a two-year-old can help put her toys away and set a table. My three-year-old son's skills with a small vacuum can put most adults to shame. (Perhaps because he is so close to the ground and can see everything.) Ten-year-olds can do almost any household chore, and should, including scrubbing the toilets and shower, washing floors, and unloading the dishwasher.

Tiny Tots at Work

Very young children, particularly the under-six crowd, will enthusiastically perform household chores that adults would consider mundane. The secret to getting very young children to work is to provide the right tools for them and give them work that is either close to the ground or safely accessible from a stool or a chair.

Montessori schools are the experts in this area. They have the two- and three-year-old children sweeping up after snack time with little handheld brooms. These same little ones are taught how to keep their snacks neatly on the table, and how to clean up a spill by themselves. They are taught how to put everything away after they use it, leaving less work for the teachers at the end of the day. The environment is the key to pulling this off successfully. In Montessori schools everything is assigned a place and the children are made aware of where everything goes.

Young children have a fascination with squirt bottles, so make sure you let them perform squirt and scrub tasks. However, don't let them use harsh commercial cleaners. Put benign mixes in the squirt bottle, like a mixture of vinegar, water, and soap, or Murphy's Oil Soap and water for hardwood floors. My children have literally come to blows over who gets the privilege of wielding the squirt bottle and Swiffer to clean the wood floors. They have learned to take turns, and my floor gets damn clean in the process.

Chores for Young Kids (Ages Two to Seven):

Setting the table for meals
Sweeping the table after meals
Washing the table after meals
Sweeping the floor under the table

Feeding pets
Vacuuming with a very lightweight vacuum (the bagless, cord-
    less Shark Quick and Quiet sweeper is only $29 and is per-
    fect for the little ones)
Some gardening
Watering plants
Anything that involves a squirt bottle and scrubbing

CHORES FOR OLDER KIDS (AGES SEVEN TO EIGHTEEN):

Washing dishes or loading/unloading dishwasher
Laundry—sorting, folding, and putting away
Cooking meals and meal planning
Washing windows
Vacuuming stairs and large rooms
Scrubbing floors
Cleaning toilets and showers
Wiping down bathroom counters and sinks

Nine Steps to Turn Your Family into a Working Family

Step 1: Make a list of all the ongoing household duties, along with how often each duty must be performed.

Step 2: If you can outsource some jobs to your husband, do so now. If he is reluctant, explain the benefits of the working family and the example it will set for your children. If that doesn't work, calmly remind him that John Wayne Bobbitt didn't do laundry either.

Step 3: Decide which chores the children will be responsible for. A good rule of thumb (to start) is to assign three chores per child. These chores can be rotated later.

Step 4: Make a chore chart and hang it in a public space in your house. The chart should include the chores by name, the name of the person responsible, and when each job needs to be done. As each chore is completed, you can put a check mark on the chart.

Step 5: Have a family meeting to discuss the new chore chart, explaining what will be required of each child.

Step 6: Offer some incentive to the kids. Whether it's an allowance, or privileges, or whatever, there has to be something in it for them. Or you can classify the chores into "must do regardless, just because you live here" and "work for reward" categories. Cleaning your own bedroom, for example, would be a "must do" chore that has no reward (because essentially the kids are taking care of their own stuff) while scrubbing toilets or feeding the cat could be a "work for pay" chore that warrants an allowance.

Step 7: Provide the necessary supplies, and demonstrate how you want the chore to be done.

Step 8: Initially, monitor the chores as they're being done to offer encouragement and suggestions. Don't reprimand the kids as they're working, and don't smother them. Let them figure some of it out for themselves.

Step 9: Give positive feedback immediately. Memorize at least a dozen compliments to use for a job well done, such as:

Wow, that is one clean floor!
Impressive job on the dishes, honey.
I appreciate your hard work in the garden today.
You are a terrific helper! Thank you.
Wow, your toys are put away so neatly!
You did a very thorough job vacuuming.
I like how you cleaned the windows. They look great.
Your dolls look happy to have such a tidy bed.

Taking It "in House"

If you find yourself in the position of having to slash your household budget, reassess all of the jobs that you normally pay to have done someplace else or by someone else.

For example, do you really need to pay for a gym membership when you can get an amazing workout at home? I have a friend who recently ditched the gym in favor of an at-home web-based workout, and she's in better shape than ever.

How about personal grooming? Try cutting and coloring your own hair. Sharon Stone has been doing it for years. It's not rocket science, people. More and more women's magazines are touting the benefits of at-home grooming and offer detailed instructions on how to go about it.

DIY entertainment can be rewarding and fun as well. You can forgo expensive nights out and teach yourself chess (or piano, knitting, digital photography, etc.) instead. At-home entertainment can be just as fun as going out, depending on how creative and motivated you are.

RECESSION HEAT INDEX

	SMOKIN' HOT	TEPID	CHILLED
Produce	Backyard mini-farm	Locally grown	Organic
Car repairs	Sourcing parts on eBay	Local auto mechanic	Dealership
Playtime	Homemade toys	Sony PSP	Bratz dolls
Summer plans	Kid works as a Chinese tour guide	Kid hangs out at home or gets an ordinary summer job	You finance your kid's European party adventure
Fine cuisine	Teaching your kids to cook for you	Catering your own party	Personal chef

13

Working Your Contacts

It's Not "Using People," I Promise!

NETWORKING

Having a network of people to help you, and who can benefit from your help, is vital during a recession. Now is the time to spend more time than usual on networking. If you or your husband gets laid off, your network can help you find a new job or develop some other income stream.

SIX SECRETS TO BEEFING UP YOUR NETWORK

1. Build authentic relationships with people you genuinely want to associate with. Think of ways you can benefit them and who can benefit from your help. The best network is a great circle of friends.

2. Volunteer with organizations that you care about, and develop relationships with like-minded people.

3. Stay visible—you want to be seen as an expert, or at least

a strong resource, in one particular area. People will come to you for advice, help, or referral, which keeps you visible and on their minds.

4. Develop a ten-second "elevator pitch" about yourself and what you do. You need to be able to convey in just a few sentences what you do and why you're different from everyone else.

5. Follow up. Don't let the people you encounter slip away. Always follow up with a quick phone message or e-mail. This shows that you are willing to forge a relationship.

6. Learn how to work a room. Dale Carnegie's *How to Win Friends and Influence People* is still the bible on this topic.

Know Your Neighbors

Okay, I'll fess up. I'm the type of person who loves it when my friends and neighbors come knocking at my door unannounced. If they just walk in without ringing the doorbell, that's even better. Is this normal? Probably not. I love the fact that I can have toys and meatballs and dirty socks strewn from one end of my house to the next, and my neighbors love me anyway. But it wasn't always like this.

In our old neighborhood, I once threw a neighborhood holiday bash at my home in an attempt to get to know my neighbors better. I took a map of our neighborhood, drew a reasonable-size circle around our house, and invited everyone who resided in the circle. Surprisingly, most of the people did not know one another even though they lived just a few steps away. This baffled me, because they all seemed like nice, normal people who made friends easily.

Why are we so distant from our neighbors? It might be lack of time. People work more and are at home less. Those who work from home stay inside. Another factor is that most of our suburban landscape is designed so that we have to drive everywhere, instead of walking or taking public transportation.

The reasons are many, I'm sure. But I for one thrive on a sense of community and I suspect there are many other people who do, too. In a weak economy, knowing your neighbors is very important. You will need them and they will need you. Having a support system with people who reside in your immediate proximity will benefit you, and not just emotionally. Your neighbors can help get you out of a jam, and you probably have skills that can help them as well.

Community can provide social support by offering continuity, stability, and a sense of group responsibility that benefits everyone—especially children.

PERSPECTIVE CHECK FROM THE GREAT DEPRESSION

ℰℓℊ

"Life was simple, friends and neighbors cared about one another."

—*Vera Lindsay, Mondovi, Wisconsin.*

From *Stories and Recipes of the Great Depression of the 1930's* by Rita Van Amber (see Resources).

NINE PRACTICAL TIPS FOR GETTING TO KNOW YOUR NEIGHBORS

1. Take a walk every day. Vary the time of your walks so you can see different people each time. Say hello.

2. Visit your neighborhood park, especially if you have kids or a dog. Strike up a conversation with the other adults. Have a little piece of paper tucked in your pocket so you can write down names.

3. Get outside and work in the yard. Vegetable gardening has a way of attracting the interest of neighbors and sparking conversation.

4. Have a garage sale. Put out lots of signs and watch the neighbors pour in. Remember to write down names.

5. Host a neighborhood potluck. The Fourth of July is a great time to do this.

6. Get together with some other neighborhood residents and pitch a "progressive dinner" party, where people go from one house to the next for each course.

7. Start a neighborhood group that meets monthly, like a poker or bridge group, or a reading or investment club.

8. Bake something for a neighbor who just moved in, just had a baby, or just because.

9. Hire neighborhood kids to babysit for you. You'll get to know their parents better and get introduced to more neighbors.

PERSPECTIVE CHECK FROM
THE GREAT DEPRESSION

ɔℓϱ

"[At four years of age], Milo [Olson] remembers his mother
after church asking a neighbor friend how they were
getting along. When she learned they had no food at all,
Mrs. Olson invited them to dinner. Home from church,
Mr. Olson quickly changed his clothes and went out to
look over the flock of chickens. He selected the one most
likely not to be laying much longer, chopped its head off,
stripped the feathers off, and brought it to Mrs. Olson. By
the time the guests arrived, they were met by the succulent
aroma of a roast chicken dinner with all the trimmings
that the times permitted."

From *Stories and Recipes of the Great Depression of the 1930's* by
Rita Van Amber (see Resources).

COMMUNITY GROUPS AND CHURCH

Think of community groups like an extended family. You are
likely to forge solid and long-term relationships with people
you meet in community groups because chances are you will
have something in common with these people. Community
groups, like neighbors, are vital during hard times. Some
groups you might join include

- Language club
- Churches, synagogues, etc.
- Groups for playing cards

- Volunteer organizations
- Knitting and sewing clubs (Don't laugh, it's cool to know how to sew! If the recession quashes your designer clothing addiction, you will still be able to create a fabulous knock-off Diane von Furstenberg wrap dress.)

RECESSION HEAT INDEX			
	SMOKIN' HOT	TEPID	CHILLED
Mental wellness	Talking to your neighbors	Talking through your computer avatar	Talking to your therapist
Philanthropy	Feeding your neighbors	Saving the polar bears	Saving the whales
Musical outlet	Playing real instruments with real people	Guitar Hero	MTV

14

Second Income Opportunities

Starting a Business or Recession-Proofing the One You Have

Ironically, starting a business in a recession is actually a good idea. It's like vacationing in the off-season—it's less crowded and everything is on sale. Why were there more self-made millionaires created during the Great Depression than during the Roaring Twenties? The 1920s had a bull market caused by excessive credit. Most money was being made by stock and real estate speculation rather than true value creation. When the economy entered into deflation in the 1930s, those who could create value were able to capture it because their savings and profits were not inflated away. I believe we will experience a similar situation as the United States enters a prolonged recession.

A key point to remember is that even if the U.S. economy suffers a severe depression and the economy contracts 30%, as it did during the Great Depression, people will still need food, shelter, transportation, movies, clothing, etc. Much of that 30% contraction during the Great Depression was from banking industry excesses and malfeasance during the 1920s. The real economy—based on the stuff we eat, buy, watch, and drink—still chugged along, and in that realm, great fortunes were made.

The last two decades have been very good to the banking industry in this country. Low interest rates and easy money from the Federal Reserve have allowed banks to take speculative risks with few consequences. I believe the tide is shifting, and rather abruptly. Profits will once again come from hard work and creating value, not just flipping stocks or houses.

During a recession, established businesses tend to retrench and focus on protecting what they have, rather than invest in innovation to take on new markets. After the dot-com implosion in Seattle and after 9/11, business actually became much easier to conduct because the speculative mania had moved out of the market temporarily. In addition, the competition acted a bit like a deer caught in headlights, frozen in place, making it easier for those willing to move to excel. Unfortunately, Mr. Greenspan, the former Federal Reserve chairman, quickly created a new bubble in housing, and the market became noisy with delusions of grandeur once again.

Cash Flow Is King

This next recession will be a great time either to start a business or to buy a business, as long as it's the right type of business. The key, though, is to focus on cash flow. Going forward, businesses will be valued far more for their ability to generate profits now than on some new widget that could someday generate profits. You do not want to be dependent on having to raise capital for your business, because the climate will become very difficult for doing so. Focus on businesses that generate profits from the get-go and not businesses that require large amounts of investment before they can generate a positive return.

Six Reasons to Start a Business During a Recession

1. There is less competition. During economic boom times, there seem to be five serious start-ups for every great business idea. During a recession, far fewer will be there to tough it out, leaving you with ample market share.

2. The hungriest wolves hunt the best. The recession will force you, as a business owner, to act faster and smarter, and to be more aggressive in pushing your business to success.

3. Recessions are a good time to add new customers, for two reasons. First, your competitors might not be managing their businesses well and might not be able to adjust fast enough to the new economic climate. Those businesses will fail, allowing you to pick up their customers. Second, your potential customers will be examining every possible way to cut costs. If you can offer better pricing than their current vendors, you can win their business.

4. Contract manufacturers want your business. You can negotiate more favorable payment terms and lower order minimums with contract manufacturers during a recession because they need your business. So if you decide to start a product company, contract manufacturers will be more willing to help you out.

5. You'll be ready for the rebound. If you set up your business during a recession, it gives you time to correct mistakes, refine your sales pitch, and build a customer base. Once the economy starts picking up again, you'll be in a fantastic growth position.

6. It's much easier to find quality employees. Unemployment can grow dramatically during a recession, so it will be easier to find top-notch, cost-effective talent, as well as to retain that talent.

Starting your own business is a thrilling experience, but it can also be a bit intimidating. The intimidation comes from fear of the unknown. It's not nearly as hard as most people think, though. In fact, women now are starting the majority of new businesses.

This makes sense when you think about it. Women control 80% of the purchases in the United States. They generally know much more than their male counterparts about consumer trends and what kids or women want. We women are survivors, and the businesses we own survive. According to the National Women's Business Council's website, women-owned businesses are just as likely to stay in business as their male-owned counterparts—75.1% are likely to stay in business after three years. Women-owned businesses are also far less likely to have to lay off employees, thus making them better employers.

The first thing to do is to think about a product that fills a need. For inspiration, watch *The Big Idea* with Donny Deutsch on CNBC. He does a great job profiling successful start-ups. Most are simple ideas that make you slap yourself on the forehead and say, "I should have thought of that."

To start a business, you need to identify a product and then a market for it. If you are not the creative type, look at a market that's missing something another market has. Many a successful business has been created by bringing a unique product to the U.S. market from overseas. With the U.S. dollar in the toilet, there are great opportunities to take some of the new products in the U.S. to overseas markets.

STRUTTING THE CATWALK FOR EUROS, NOT BENJAMINS

Here's a kick in the pants to anyone who incorrectly links beauty and low IQ: late in 2007, Bloomberg News reported that the world's richest supermodel, Gisele Bündchen, preferred to be paid in euros rather than U.S. dollars. At the time, those who don't follow economics didn't understand why she would take such a strong stance and make a public proclamation about the USD. Since her decision, the U.S. dollar has plunged by almost 15%.

Gisele has it right. Get your income (or at least some of it) out of U.S. dollars. That's right, ladies, when it comes to income, it's time to think outside the box. I mean way outside the box. Outside the country, actually. While the U.S. might be strapped for cash, it is freely flowing in other parts of the world. There are many ways to take advantage of this, which are discussed in the last chapter.

BRINGING BACK "MADE IN THE U.S.A."

The U.S. has changed from being a country of manufacturers to one of service providers. If the dollar continues its precipitous decline and shipping costs continue to escalate, that trend will reverse. In 2001, the cost of shipping a container from China to the U.S. was $3,000. In 2008, it is $8,000. If oil hits $200 a barrel (by 2010, according to projections), shipping costs will be $15,000. In 2002, containers were shipped back empty to China from the U.S. During the first quarter of

2008, freight volumes from China to the U.S. have dropped by 15%, and it is extremely difficult to find an empty container to ship to China because the trade flow has reversed. Tragically, we're not shipping manufactured goods, but rather raw materials for Chinese manufacturers. However, some companies are now relocating their manufacturing back to the United States because costs overseas are making the U.S. market more competitive.

A deep, prolonged recession will likely force America to manufacture its own products once again, and to export them. Our manufacturing base will have to be rebuilt. It will be a difficult process, but we Americans are nothing if not resourceful and adaptable.

Those of us who face the challenge of establishing manufacturing will be the cream that rises to the top during this recession. Why?

- People need stuff. Not services but actual tangible things—pencils, cars, electronics, plastics, lamps, shoes, dried cherries, everything.

- Our devalued dollar means that U.S. manufacturers will be in a great position to export their products overseas.

- Prices for imported goods will surge as the dollar collapses and shipping costs increase, giving U.S. manufacturers an advantage with U.S. customers.

- There will be a glut of people with service-related job experience, as opposed to experience in nuts-and-bolts manufacturing. Many service jobs and businesses will be eliminated. There will be too much competition in the services arena.

Start Manufacturing Something

If you're starting from scratch with a brand-new business, you should seriously consider making a product—a tangible, physical product. Not a service business (spa, restaurant, or business service) but a product that you own the exclusive rights to; a product that you are responsible for manufacturing yourself or that a contract manufacturer makes for you.

Service Businesses

For the most part, service-based businesses could be in serious trouble during a recession. There are exceptions, of course. Some service businesses could thrive or at least survive during the recession. Examples of these types of service businesses are those that

- Cater to tourists
- Cater to ultra-wealthy Americans (they won't be affected by the recession as much and will still be spending money)
- Fix things (cars, houses, etc.)
- Cater to discount retailers like Costco and Target, provided those retailers can still sell at a low cost and keep their customers
- Educate children, because parents will still be sacrificing to provide the best possible opportunities for their kids
- Are in the medical industry, provided insurance companies are still solvent and government entitlement medical programs don't go bankrupt
- Have the U.S. military as a customer (or another government wing with big spending power)

There are other types of service businesses that will also do well. However, the United States is exiting out of the service industry era. If you presently own a service business, especially a business whose customers could easily cut your service in a cash crunch, then it's time to do some serious thinking about ways to diversify your income. Try to think of ways to incorporate a product into your service-based business. For example, if you own a salon, you might consider releasing a DIY hair care video or creating a new hair product.

Manufacturing a product, especially one that's exportable, can be your key to thriving during this recession.

What Types of Products?

Consider making a product that is shippable (exportable), even though shipping costs are high. Remember that, on a relative basis, things are becoming cheaper in America, so you might have an advantage as an exporter. Small, lightweight items, like informational DVDs and CDs, are easy to ship or airfreight overseas. These types of products also have huge profit margins because they're so cheap to produce.

Consider products that Americans need (not ones they want). Think about essentials like food, transportation, shoes, home heating, appliances, and alcohol (not a need, but it is popular to consume in a recessionary environment). Other products that will do well are those that you can ship overseas to meet consumer demand. Think about fashion and beauty products, because working women abroad have money to spend, and they want to look good, just like us.

Don't be scared. Think of a product, hit the local library, and figure out how to make it. Ask some industry old-timers. Retirees generally love to share advice, so don't forget to seek them out and pick their brains.

Try to choose a product that you can make locally, if possible. Making your product in your house might be cheap and convenient, but sometimes that's not realistic. You can find a contract manufacturer in your local area to help you progress from the sample-making phase all the way to full production. Because business is slower during a recession, you might be pleasantly surprised by the favorable terms you're able to negotiate for yourself. In fact, if your product is good enough, a manufacturer might even be willing to back you financially.

Once your product is developed, constantly look for ways to make it better, of higher quality, and more cheaply.

EXPORTING

Exporting is a fancy term for taking goods made in the United States and shipping them to other countries. It sounds complicated, but it's really quite simple. In fact, most exporters are small businesses, and the number of small- to medium-size U.S. exporters is presently only 230,000.

Exporting is one area of the U.S. economy that's benefiting in a huge way from the tanking U.S. dollar. A number of U.S. politicians and business leaders are hoping that exports will be the nation's savior by staving off a massive recession. We'll certainly keep our fingers crossed.

Whether or not it has any immediate impact on the recession, one thing is for sure: U.S. exporters are seeing a huge jump in business now, and this trend will continue. As a May 2008 *Financial Times* article professed, as long as emerging economies keep on growing (as are China and areas that are really exploding), the U.S. export market will grow as well. This is true whether or not the dollar rebounds. U.S. exporters are taking this to the bank, and you can too.

Being an exporter is easier than ever, thanks to electronic commerce. You can sell your product overseas without stepping out of your home or changing out of your pajamas (but please, at least put on a bra before the FedEx guy shows up). It can be as simple as selling on eBay and offering international shipping or as complicated as manufacturing your own product, stuffing thousands of your widgets in a cargo container, and letting them set sail for destinations abroad.

Think about what people in other countries might want or need, particularly in emerging markets in Asia, where the middle class is rising quickly. Pay attention to magazine and Internet articles that discuss daily life and trends in these markets. For example, a recent Associated Press article stated that half of Filipino women, 41% of Malaysian women, and 45% of Hong Kong women use a skin-whitening product. I know several Indian women who claim that skin-whitening creams are used widely in India as well. There is a huge market here: women who want to lighten their skin. What kinds of products can you sell to this customer? Supplements? An informational video? Self-hypnosis CDs to achieve the lightest skin possible? The possibilities are numerous. Open your mind and brainstorm ideas based on the trends.

And remember, just because a particular product hasn't yet been introduced to a country doesn't mean consumers there don't want it. Many developing nations are just beginning to experience some of America's luxuries—Ben & Jerry's, paparazzi, designer condoms . . .

Teaming with a U.S. manufacturer that does not presently export is another way to become an exporter. The manufacturer makes the product, and you handle the sales effort overseas. It doesn't matter whether your strategy is to sell the product internationally online or to international retailers. The bottom line is that the manufacturer will like the extra revenues and you will capture your percentage from all the business you generate overseas. If you go this route, be sure to protect yourself by being the only point of contact for customers, and get an exclusive distribution deal, in writing, so that you can't be cut out of the picture.

For more information, check out www.export.gov, which has an extensive list of websites and information for businesses planning international sales strategies. The U.S. Chamber of Commerce also offers a "trade toolkit" that allows you to search for data on the country of your choice. You need to register to get full access on its website (www.uschamber.com), but use of the site is free.

SELLING STUFF TO WEALTHY FOREIGNERS

If the dollar continues to slide, and especially if there's some major economic event, there will be a glut of secondhand consumer goods that can be purchased for practically nothing. When people get into serious financial trouble, they're forced to sell belongings like boats, furniture, TVs, computers, jewelry, etc. This could happen as people lose their jobs or find themselves unable to keep up with a new adjustable-rate mortgage payment. Sad, but true.

You could buy this stuff and hang onto it for resale, or broker deals with foreigners who will be coming in to do bargain shopping. It won't be uncommon for cargo ships to be sent overseas with all the consumer goods that Americans are trying to sell. Do you know anything about antiques? American antiques are especially desirable to foreigners, and this could be a good business during a recession era. Anything with steel or other natural resources as main components will also be in demand.

CATERING TO THE TOURIST

The United States is seeing a record number of foreigners arriving on our shores for travel and bargain shopping. People worldwide still love to travel to popular U.S. tourist destinations like the Grand Canyon, Disney World, Maui, Washington, D.C., San Francisco, and New York City. With our dollar devaluating, we're going to see more and more tourists looking for cheap stuff and services and a good time. Reporter Michael A. Fletcher pointed out in a *Washington Post* article published May 9, 2008, that tourism is surging in the U.S. In January 2008, we had 3.4 million visitors. That's an 11% bump over the previous January. In New York, hotel occupancy and sales of tickets to Broadway plays are up. In 2007 alone, foreign tourists spent $122 billion in the United States.

Chinese tourists will flood into the United States in large numbers if we open our doors to them, as Europe has. Time will tell whether our government will loosen visa standards and allow the Chinese to come in freely and spend their money here. The number of Chinese travelers worldwide is astronomical. Remember back in the 1980s when it was a cliché to see Japanese tourists in America feverishly snapping images with their cameras? Well, Japanese tourists will seem like a tiny blip on the tourism radar compared to the Chinese. Watch out, Maui! Look out, Disneyland! Prepare for the invasion.

If you live near a popular tourist destination, start thinking of creative ways to cater to these customers. Can you make an appealing product? Sell a product to cruise ships? Learn one or two foreign languages and cater to non-English-speaking foreigners? What might tourists need that you can supply?

CELEBRITIES AND ENTERTAINMENT

Another thing we still have going for us in America is our celebrity culture. Our celebrities are worshipped worldwide, and this will not be affected by the recession. Interest in movies and television will likely be stronger than ever, just as it was for movies during the Great Depression, when people sought inexpensive escapes from reality.

One way to "make bank" off this worldwide obsession is to manufacture a product that's worn by or used by celebrities. I'm not talking about paying millions to have a celebrity endorse your product. I'm talking about simply having them own it. Think about it from a consumer's standpoint. Would you rather own a killer pair of shoes just like the ones Gwyneth Paltrow chose to wear out on the town, or like a pair she was paid to endorse in a magazine ad? Obviously, consumers want the design she wore out to dinner, because it's more authentic. The consumer is wising up to advertisements.

To illustrate this point more vividly, a friend of mine from Taiwan was at my house one recent morning, and we started talking about my fashion jewelry business. She nearly spit her soy milk all over my kitchen when I rattled off the list of celebrities who wear my jewelry. She explained to me that some of the most respected celebrities in Asia are in fact American actors and singers. She hopped on the computer and showed me a Taiwanese gossip website, and sure enough, Angelina Jolie was on the home page.

Once you build up a little list of celebrities who have your product, you'll be ready to start exporting and getting publicity offshore. The U.S. celebrity factor carries a lot of weight internationally, and it just might open doors for you abroad. So if you want to get your handmade hemp and leather handbags into some major retail chain in Brazil or Shanghai, make sure that Jennifer Aniston has one first. (Oh, and for the last time, will you please learn a foreign language like Portuguese, Russian, or Mandarin?)

If you want more information on how to contact celebrities, check out www.whorepresents.com. I also recommend checking out productivity expert Tim Ferriss's book *The 4-Hour Workweek,* which contains a lot of useful information about approaching celebrities and very successful people. This book is also packed with great business ideas, as well as how to evaluate what kind of business to start. I honestly cannot recommend it enough.

𝒥UICY BITS

Hot industries for U.S.-based business

Medical

Government

Security

Alcohol and tobacco

Energy and alternative energy

Food and other necessary consumables

Agriculture

Exports

Academia/education

BARGAIN SHOPPING: BUYING A BUSINESS

Many private equity investment experts expect the purchase price for privately held companies to drop by 50% after 2010. Currently, privately held businesses are, on average, valued at six times their EBITDA (earnings before interest, taxes, depreciation, and amortization). So, if a company makes $1 million a year, you can buy it for $6 million. Obviously this will vary by industry and circumstance.

After 2010, as baby boomers rush to retire, their businesses flood the market, and investment capital dries up, that same business may be valued at $3 million. There will be many excellent opportunities to either buy or start businesses during the next decade. There will be more businesses sold in the next five years than were sold during the last two hundred years. The largest generation in the history of the United States is retiring, and many of these successful business owners do not know what to do with their companies. Their kids have grown up in a coddled environment and would rather just spend their parents' money than earn it. In fact, the vast majority of business owners do not turn their companies over to their children. This means there will be many great opportunities to buy a business for a bargain. In fact, for smaller businesses, you'll likely be able to negotiate owner financing so you won't even have to put up a lot of money. Most of the owners just want to stop working so hard and will be ecstatic to turn the business over to someone who can carry the torch.

It's beyond the scope of this book to explain how to buy a business, so hit your local library. There is an abundance of books on the subject. The key is to be aware of opportunity and keep your eyes open. You'll be amazed how many opportunities you'll find.

RECESSION HEAT INDEX			
	SMOKIN' HOT	TEPID	CHILLED
Language	Learning Mandarin	Learning Spanish	Learning French
Business goal	Positive cash flow	Revenues over profits	Clicks over revenues
Mom-and-pop shop	Pawnshop	Nail salon	Flower shop
New business	Exporter/ manufacturer	Organizational consultant	Doggy boutique

15

Where We Stuffed Our Money

Strange or Savvy?

One of the questions women ask me most frequently is, "What are you investing in?" This strikes me as a funny question because I'm not a financial adviser or broker or doing work related to the finance industry at all. But being married to an economics geek has certainly had its advantages. We've made our money decisions based on economics, not the advice of financial planners. Therefore, our approach is unconventional—and sometimes entertaining.

Investing in anything is a crapshoot. Even having your money in a bank is a crapshoot (as in the Great Depression, when banks went belly-up). Really, investing is just one big gamble. Sometimes you win, and sometimes you lose. Just make the smartest decisions you can and go from there. The point of this book is to give you the tools and information to make your own decisions, to thrive financially during a recession (or any other time), and to enjoy the emotional benefits of having enough.

If you are out of debt and have money saved or invested, you should pay attention to where your money is right now. Your investment strategy could mean the difference between losing almost everything or coming out of the recession wealthy. If you are married and your husband normally handles your investments, have him read this chapter, then sit down and make some joint decisions.

DISCLAIMER

We are not licensed certified financial advisers (CFAs), lawyers, accountants, or any other type of finance professionals. We are not recommending that you invest as we have or follow any of our recommendations. The following details about how we have invested and what we have done are purely opinion about the best markets and places to invest. It is not a recommendation. Please do your own research and make your own decisions.

BUCKING TRADITION

THE 60–40 THEORY AND WHY IT'S ANTIQUATED

Wall Street is a well-oiled marketing machine that cares foremost about selling its products, *not* about creating value for you, the customer. Over the last twenty years, Wall Street firms have been pitching the 60–40 rule for investing. The 60–40 investment theory is that if you place 60% of your investment assets in equities (normally U.S. equities, such as Microsoft and General Electric) and 40% in fixed income (again, normally U.S. bonds), then you will get the best overall returns. This theory was pioneered by Harry Markowitz, Merton Miller, and William Sharpe, and they won a Nobel Prize in economics for it in 1990, a fact that every financial adviser will cite to back up how great the theory is.

The problem is that the theory was completed in the 1960s and was based on only ten years of data collected during the 1950s. The 1950s enjoyed the greatest bull market in the history of the United States. In fact, the 60–40 theory has worked in only two decades over the last eighty years: the 1950s and the 1980s. Both were giant bull markets with steadily decreasing interest rates. (Even a broken watch is correct twice a day.)

Markowitz and Sharpe recently admitted publicly that this is *not* the ideal investment strategy for today. At the time they formulated it, it was cutting-edge and brilliant. But now there are much better ways of investing. If investors had followed this model during the 1970s, they would have gotten crushed.

Yet Wall Street still loves the 60–40 investment strategy because it is simple and easy to communicate, and a good percentage of financial advisers are still pushing this archaic strategy on their clientele. Don't get me wrong—it's generally better than all bonds or all equities, but the ratio is rather arbitrary.

Both the public and Wall Street have started to wake up to this fact, so the financial houses have come up with a new sales gimmick.

100 Minus Your Age

The latest marketing shtick is the allocation of investments based on the following formula: Take your age and subtract it from 100. This is the percentage that should be invested in equities, and the remainder should go into bonds. So if you're 43 years old, you should have 57% (100 - 43) of your investments in equities and the remainder, 43%, invested in bonds.

The premise of the theory is that as you get older, you should invest more conservatively, into fixed income (bonds). Yet this theory is even more arbitrary than the 60–40 theory. At least the 60–40 theory had a decade of data to support it. This new theory makes for a great sales pitch, but it's unfounded.

Here's an equally absurd theory (though probably more lucrative), courtesy of yours truly: take the measurement between your ass and your elbow in inches, multiply by ten, buy that number of gold coins, and put them in an Australian gold account.

I cringe every time the "100 minus your age" agenda is pushed on popular women's-television shows and in magazines. The financial experts who tout this popular gimmick are tacitly admitting they have no theories of their own and haven't a clue about economics. More important, it is dangerous misinformation that could push the elderly straight into poverty. Following this advice, they would put the bulk of their wealth into U.S. bonds. But if U.S. bonds collapse, they could lose everything. Grannies beware.

Buy and Hold . . . Then Say Your Prayers

Wall Street firms strongly recommend that you buy and hold your investments. I strongly disagree. Markets change over time, and this change is accelerating. Microsoft was and is a great company. However, if you bought its stock in late 1999 and held it until today, you would have lost almost 50% in stock value, and if you take into account true inflation, your total loss would be 75%. If you bought stocks at the market peak in 1929, you wouldn't have broken even until 1944, not counting inflation. In 1989, the Japanese Nikkei stock exchange peaked at over 40,000. Japan is still the second-largest economy in the world, but the Nikkei is at 14,000 today. Maybe in another twenty years it will get back to where it was.

This strategy serves Wall Street managers well because your money will be stuck in a mutual fund for them to handle. Why do 80% of mutual funds underperform the market indices each year? Because the majority of investment advisers and fund managers are far better salesmen than they are money managers.

However, I'm not saying you should day-trade or rotate your portfolio every couple of weeks. My family evaluates our investments a couple times a year and makes changes based on observations and research. There are really good money managers and financial advisers out there, and they are worth their weight in gold. We use an investment adviser ourselves who has made exceptional returns for us over the last several years. But before you choose one, please research thoroughly, and verify references and the history of returns before you sign up.

A Joint Decision

Every financial decision and investment is a joint decision by the two adults in our house. We bounce ideas off each other. We talk about the pros and cons of different investments (including the sale of our house). Every major financial decision involves both of us, not just one or the other. This is a very important point, and one that I believe strengthens our marriage. When both parties are involved in the decision making, there's no finger pointing if an investment goes down in value. Likewise, if an investment happens to skyrocket, you can both enjoy the rewards (although I do like to remind Dan that I was the one who insisted on buying precious metals back in the spring of 2007—a henpecking that resulted in a lovely financial gain).

Our Money

Our investment strategy is a bit different from most other people's. We own a couple of small businesses based in Seattle. My husband's business, which manages the distribution centers for several large U.S. companies, is dependent upon the U.S. economy and the health of the consumer. He has taken steps to help protect it from the cyclical downturn we expect, but because his customers are here in the United States, there is only so much he can do. For our investment portfolio, we consider the ownership of our businesses to be our main exposure to the U.S. economy. If the U.S. economy rebounds and does well, then our businesses should do well. If the economy goes into a deep recession, as we think it might, then the success of our businesses could be adversely impacted.

Therefore, we have allocated our remaining assets overseas. We have liquidated all residential and commercial real estate and, except for a small investment account, liquidated all U.S. stocks and bonds. We have spread our investments across the following various asset classes:

Resource Stocks

A good portion of our portfolio is invested in companies that farm, mine, or drill for natural resources such as timber, gold, copper, oil, and natural gas. We have invested mainly in foreign producers to take advantage of the devaluing dollar, but we do have some holdings in high-quality U.S. gold and silver mining companies. We are in agreement with Jim Rogers, the famous investor and cofounder, with George Soros, of the Quantum Fund, that commodities still have a long bull market ahead of them and that companies that produce those commodities should continue to do well. We have been very pleased with Global Resource Investments (www.gril.net) and

Doug Casey Research for finding high-quality international resource stocks.

BRIC AND ASIAN ETFs

BRIC stands for Brazil, Russia, India, and China. ETF is an exchange-traded fund and a lower-cost way to purchase equities based on a specific country or industry sector. China has the potential by 2020 to replace the United States as the world's largest economic power. Russia, if its economic growth continues, could have the world's highest per capita income in fifteen years. All four countries have experienced incredible growth in this decade—Brazil and Russia because of their depth of natural resources, China because of its manufacturing ability and huge population, and India because of its large middle class and dynamic technology economy. Over the long term, these four major economies plus the smaller Asian economies will likely continue to be major growth engines for the world economy. Their populations are young, hungry, and willing to sacrifice for the future. Their economies run strong trade and budget surpluses. Long-term investments in the BRIC countries should pay off handsomely. Over the short term, they are vulnerable to the credit crisis and emerging-markets equity bubbles.

FOREIGN HIGH-DIVIDEND INVESTMENT TRUSTS

Cash flow is king. There are several high-quality foreign income trusts that pay dividends in low double digits, specifically Canadian oil trusts. And if you trust that the price of oil will continue to climb and the dollar will continue to depreciate, you can receive capital gains growth and currency gains as well. Euro Pacific Capital (www.europac.net), run by Peter Schiff, specializes in this form of investment.

Foreign High-Quality Fixed Income (Bonds)

No matter what you think about Dick Cheney, he is pretty good at making money. In his financial statements, he disclosed that he has $25 million invested in high-quality European bonds. I wonder if he knew something that we didn't! European interest rates are higher and their currency has appreciated over 50% against the U.S. dollar since 2001. For fixed-income investments, now is probably not the time to invest in U.S. debt (bonds). Interest rates are again at almost record low levels and inflation is boiling over. The Federal Reserve will likely have no choice but to begin increasing interest rates soon. This will have a negative impact on bond prices and hurt returns.

Gold and Silver

We have a variety of gold and silver investments. A small percentage of our assets is invested in gold and silver as a hedge against inflation, and we also believe that gold and silver prices will continue to rise in value. There are many ways to own gold and silver, and here are a few.

1. A great resource is Jim Turk's www.goldmoney.com. Jim Turk is highly respected in the investment community and has been a gold advocate for many years. His service allows you to purchase precious metals that are held for you in secure vaults in the Channel Islands and Switzerland.

2. The Perth Mint is an Australian, government-backed mint. It has been around for 100 years. The accounts are guaranteed by the Australian government, and also insured by Lloyd's of London. Perth Mint stores the gold and silver that you buy, and the storage is free. You can get a Perth

Mint account at www.europac.net. This is a very safe way
to own gold and silver.

3. Physical ownership. If you decide to buy precious metal
   coins, you will notice that it now takes six months for
   delivery, if you can even get them. To purchase coins, just
   do a search for coin galleries in your local area. You can
   also go to Monex or Kitco to purchase them on the Internet. As demand continues to rise, it is very possible that
   you may not be able to purchase coins or precious metal
   bullion in the future. Before you invest in gold and silver
   coins, be aware that the government can change the rules
   and make it illegal to possess bullion. Just recently, in an
   effort to stabilize its economy, Vietnam made it illegal to
   import gold.

4. Gold and silver stocks. Kitco lists the top gold and silver
   stocks.

A Lesson in History

From: President of the United States
      Franklin Delano Roosevelt
To: The United States Congress
Dated: 5 April 1933

Presidential Executive Order 6102

"I, Franklin D. Roosevelt, President of the United States of America, do declare that said national emergency still continues to exist and pursuant to said section do hereby prohibit the hoarding of gold coins, gold bullion, and gold certificates within the continental United States by individuals, partnerships, associations, and corporations and hereby prescribe the following regulations for carrying out the purposes of the order. . . ."

During the Great Depression, the U.S. Government confiscated all gold from the people in order to pay its debts to foreign governments. Precious metals are an excellent hedge against inflation, but governments are unpredictable in times of duress.

Stocks of Foreign Companies

There are still good U.S. companies to invest in, but they are getting harder to find. My husband and I are staying away from most business sectors that are dependent on the credit system: financial and banking, retail, automotive manufacturing, and residential and commercial construction. We're instead investing in companies that have a strong global presence and a good export business. Most U.S. companies' valuations will be adversely affected by the devaluation of the U.S. dollar, but those with a global footprint and producers of natural resources (energy, metals, and food commodities) should do better.

One of the challenges of investing in U.S. companies is that stocks offered by those of the highest quality (e.g., Google) are often overvalued, so it's hard to justify investing in them. There are many high-quality foreign companies priced at 30% to 50% of U.S. companies relative to earnings and growth. Add to that the devaluating U.S. dollar, and it's hard to argue that the U.S. is the place to be.

RECESSION AND BEYOND

Smart investing during the recession is great, but after that . . . then what? Since the crystal ball is in the shop, we're making plans according to what economics geeks call "future trend theories." There are many, but we've weeded out the less useful ones and pared the list down to three very relevant theories that make the most sense.

FUTURE TREND THEORY—THREE TOP PICKS

1. We are strong believers in economic and demographic cycle theory. Demographic theory tracks the size of various age groups, their spending habits by age, and their effect on the economy; and cycle theory states that history repeats itself. The practical side of me likes to pick apart these theories. I believe that just because it happened in the past doesn't mean it will happen again. Still, Dan loves charts and numbers, and this leads to an endless source of fun debate in our household. Harry Dent does a superb job

in his books and on his website, www.hsdent.com, explaining the multiple cycles that are converging simultaneously in the U.S. and global economies.

2. William Strauss and Neil Howe, in *The Fourth Turning*, discuss generational cycles. I think it's a little boring and numbers-oriented, but Dan insists it's a keeper.

3. Peter Schiff's *Crash Proof: How to Profit from the Coming Economic Collapse* details the current political and financial mess in the United States. I absolutely love Peter's book, and I have to admit, reading it (and hearing him debate on FOX News) gives me joy, mostly because he knows his stuff and has a practical solution for any bad economic news. He tells you exactly how you can weather the recession, all the while funding your designer highlights and never having to sacrifice your lifestyle. Really, what more could a girl want? Sigh.

We've scoured, dog-eared, and highlighted the above three fantastic sources and compiled them into a tidy summary for you.

Demographic Cycle

The tipping point for the boomer demographic cycle will occur in 2010. In that year, boomers will begin retiring in droves and become net consumers versus net producers for the economy. Japan had a similar demographic peak in 1989 and experienced a collapse of home values and its stock market that has lasted to this day. This demographic downturn in the United States is expected to last until the echo boomers reach their prime spending years, around 2023.

TECHNOLOGY CYCLE

Technology innovation and adoption drives huge economic change and growth. Technology follows an S-curve pattern. In the beginning, only a few brave souls venture out to spend money on new technology. (Remember the brick-size mobile phones in the 1980s.) Then the technology becomes better and cheaper and the mainstream population jumps on the bandwagon. During this phase, huge new industries are born and large amounts of money are invested and made. Then the technology matures and everyone pretty much has it already. At this point it becomes more of a commodity, and the profit margins begin to shrink. We are entering the mature commodity phase in the computer, Internet, and mobile phone technology S-curves, and the technology cycle is expected to peak at the end of this decade.

COMMODITY CYCLE

Commodities boom and bust every thirty years. The last big commodity boom occurred during the 1970s and peaked in 1980. Since 1998, commodities have been on a global tear. Gold, silver, oil, wheat, corn, soybeans, copper, and many others are at record highs. Many venerable investment experts, such as Jim Rogers, believe this cycle has much further to go because of booming demand in China and India. Harry Dent differs; he forecasts that the commodity boom will bust in 2010, as the world enters a strong deflationary period. In his opinion, the inflation cycle will peak in 2010 and then be followed by a deflationary collapse similar to the Great Depression.

WAR CYCLE

War cycles run about thirty-five to forty years. We were in Vietnam forty years ago, and seventy years ago World War II was in full bloom. It is likely that the U.S. war effort will not stop with Iraq and Afghanistan, but will further expand into the Middle East. Zbigniew Brzezinski, Barack Obama's key foreign policy adviser and national security adviser during the Carter Administration, wrote an excellent book on this topic called *The Grand Chessboard: American Primacy and Its Geostrategic Imperatives*, in which he explains that the United States needs to control oil and will use its power to get it. The fact that it was written in 1998 adds wight to Brzezinski's theories as they're borne out by current U.S. foreign policy.[1]

GENERATIONAL CYCLE

We've mentioned *The Fourth Turning*. Strauss and Howe analyzed generational cycles going back thousands of years and identified a clear, eighty-year cycle broken into twenty-year quartiles, which they call Spring, Summer, Autumn, and Winter. The authors contend that as of 2000, the U.S. entered into the Winter portion of the generational cycle. The last Winter cycle began in 1930, and in the following twenty years, the United States experienced the Great Depression and World War II.

The book is educational because it provides strong empirical data to support its case and might give you a different way to look at the world. What's fascinating is that Strauss and Howe predict the same economic upheaval that many other

---

1. Zbigniew Brzezinski, *The Grand Chessboard: American Primacy and Its Geostrategic Imperatives* (New York: Basic Books, 1998).

theorists have, but their approach is completely different. The end result is that the authors believe the next ten to fifteen years will be very difficult times for the United States. We will experience expanded warfare and economic turmoil.

CREDIT SYSTEM CYCLES

Peter Schiff, in his very readable *Crash Proof: How to Profit from the Coming Economic Collapse*, does an excellent job in detailing the current credit crisis, how we got here, and where to invest your money. It is his contention that the United States will experience simultaneous strong commodity inflation and house and stock market declines. Peter is a big proponent of investing in resource stocks, gold and silver, and foreign income trusts.

SUMMARY

Predicting the future is always a challenge, and you have to give credit to these forecasters for sticking their necks out to prognosticate on future events. History does seem to repeat itself, so the study of history and cycles can help educate investors about how to protect their assets and take advantage of opportunities. By and large, my husband and I agree with the above authors. We have invested heavily in foreign resource stocks and commodities and we have sold our U.S. real estate holdings.

The big question for us is whether the Federal Reserve will create a depression from inflation or deflation. The Great Depression was a deflationary depression and was devastating to those who held debt. Mr. Dent believes we will experience this type of economic depression and therefore recommends that when the commodity bubble bursts, investors should move their assets to high-quality bonds. Mr. Schiff and many other analysts project that the Fed will try to inflate out of our debt situation. This creates the same end result (i.e., economic depression), but in the case of inflation, you should invest your wealth in resource stocks and commodities since they tend to perform better than other assets.

Our attitude is to wait and see. In the short term, we believe the United States will experience very strong inflationary pressures, and thus resource stocks and commodities will continue to perform very well. If the Federal Reserve reacts by increasing interest rates drastically and gets aggressive on its growth of the money supply, then Mr. Dent's projection of deflation in 2010 and thereafter becomes a strong possibility. If the Fed continues its easy monetary policy, then it is likely that inflation will grow out of control and that resource-based assets will perform extraordinarily well.

Nothing is static. Things are always changing, and we will change our asset allocation as we see the need. We will be keeping a close watch on economic and political news relevant to our own investments. Please visit my website, www .practicalchic.org, for updates on where and when we are moving our money.

Asset Class Opinions

Of course, there are many other areas in which to invest— other asset classes that deserve discussion. Seek other opinions, but here are my two cents on . . .

Commercial Real Estate

The commercial real estate market has held up surprisingly well, but it should begin following the residential market off the cliff

as the economy continues to slow. If you own commercial properties that are not heavily in debt, you should be able to weather
the storm. If the property is heavily leveraged (i.e., has a large
mortgage) and vacancies rise, as they usually do during a recession, you could be in a negative cash-flow position. You may
want to consider selling the property since the general market
is, for the time being, still holding up. I believe this will soon
change, though, and commercial property prices will decline.

RESIDENTIAL REAL ESTATE

Property values have fallen and, as an aggregate, have a long
way to go. We are staying out of this market until a solid floor
is in place, which is still likely two to three years away. If you
must buy a home, look at distressed properties like foreclosures
and for owners who have to sell quickly. Lowball your offer and
hope for the best. It is very possible that home prices could still
decline an additional 40% or more. One thing to remember
is that the real estate market is a local affair, so each market
is different. Some markets have yet to decline much, whereas
others might be approaching the bottom. Do your homework
and always keep your emotions in check.

U.S. STOCKS

The tech economy is still going strong. But we agree with Mr.
Dent's analysis of the tech wave and his theory that, in late 2008,
tech stocks should resume their long-term decline from their
peak in 2000. Companies that produce resources or companies
earning a good portion of their revenue from overseas/exporting
could still be great investments. We have chosen to stay out of
U.S. stocks, except resource stocks. But in any market there are
always winners, even when the overall market is down.

U.S. BONDS

There are two components to bonds. One is the interest they pay, and the other is their face value. When interest rates are low, the price of the bond is high and the annual interest payment is low. As interest rates climb, the face value of the bond declines. Long-term bonds have interest and inflation rate expectations priced into them. If the market believes that interest rates and inflation will climb, then the face value of the bond goes down. What does this all mean? Right now, inflation is starting to rear its ugly head, and it's expected to get pretty bad over the next few years. And higher interest rates mean that everything is getting much more expensive.

Eventually, the Federal Reserve will have to respond, because the American consumer will be feeling the pain of higher price tags and increased interest rates. This means bond prices could drop precipitously. During the early 1980s, Paul Volcker, then chairman of the Federal Reserve, raised interest rates dramatically to stop inflation, and thirty-year Treasury bond face values (like a stock's share value) plummeted to around $60. By comparison, the current face value of a thirty-year T-bond is around $114.

If we have a repeat of the late 1970s and early 1980s, then you could see the current face value of bonds cut in half. If this happens, it will be bargain shopping time for bonds. The bonds might have a face value of around $60 or $70 and pay an interest rate of 10–15%, a much higher return than today's bonds.

Later, as the Fed cuts interest rates over time, not only will the face value of your bond go up but you'll also still be making the high interest rate of 10% to 15%, so you'll get a double win.

Mr. Dent believes this is the correct investment strategy after the final bubbles collapse in 2010. If the United States enters a deflationary depression, as he forecasts, we agree with this strategy, and you can bet we'll be looking at buying bonds at that time.

EMERGING MARKETS

In the long term, markets in growing nations should provide good stock returns as their economies modernize and a robust middle class forms. For the short term, their stock markets have gotten ahead of themselves. They are currently experiencing sharp corrections. Mr. Dent believes that the emerging markets are in a bubble and are starting to deflate. The Chinese stock market, after having risen over 400%, has now corrected almost 50%. One of the short-term challenges these economies face is that they are still dependent on the U.S. consumer, but that trend is quickly changing as the middle classes of Brazil, China, and India continue to grow and increase consumption. The upcoming U.S. recession should have an adverse effect on emerging markets in the near term. After the bottom sets in, though, they should provide an excellent investment opportunity. For now we are staying out of these markets.

FOREIGN STOCKS AND BONDS

These markets will likely experience the same price declines as the United States market when their central banks increase interest rates to respond to inflation. Currently, the European stock markets are suffering the same price correction that the U.S. market is. One benefit, though, is that investing abroad allows you to take advantage of appreciating foreign currencies relative to the dollar. We're avoiding companies that are heavily dependent on the U.S. economy and prefer those with strong global brands.

CURRENCIES

The debt bomb that the U.S. faces creates tremendous downward pressure on the U.S. dollar. Very smart people like Warren Buffett, Jim Rogers, Marc Faber, and Bill Gates have expressed a negative opinion of the dollar's prospects, and many of them have invested heavily abroad in either equities or currencies. It is our opinion that the U.S. dollar has a long way to go down. There are many banks now that offer savings accounts in foreign currencies. If you had put your money in euros in January 2008, you would have gained over 15% on your money in the first six months. (Actually, it's not gained; it's 15% you don't lose through the devaluation of the dollar.)

One way to look at currency is that it's the share price of the stock of a country. Issuing tons of shares without the underlying economy growing to match share growth means price eventually has to go down. For the last decade, the Federal Reserve has grown M3 (the U.S. money supply) at over 10% a year (currently over 15%).[2] Other countries' currencies have better prospects and thus could offer you a more stable place to park your savings.

RESOURCE STOCKS AND COMMODITIES

Inflation and demand that exceed supply have created a substantial global commodity boom. Companies and countries that produce these commodities should benefit greatly from this, and their stocks should perform well. This resource stock

---

2. See www.shadowstats.com; it's a great website that dissects government economic data. The U.S. Federal Reserve stopped reporting on M3 in 2007. Shadowstats re-created the M3 stats and its results closely match the Fed's.

boom should accelerate in late 2008 and run until 2010. At that point, the question will be where inflation stands. If high prices have hurt demand, then the profits of these companies will suffer and it'll be time to cash in. For the near term, according to Mr. Schiff and Mr. Dent, these companies should provide an excellent investment opportunity. After 2010, though, we're not sure. To invest in commodities, there are several new exchange-traded funds (ETFs) that allow you to buy gold, silver, oil, grains, etc., just as you would purchase a stock.

BANK ACCOUNTS

Right now you are losing money in real terms on any money that you have in a checking or savings account. Interest rates are marginal at best and inflation is running much higher, so you're actually losing purchasing power. CDs aren't any better. Try not to keep all your savings in these types of investments unless you believe everything else will go down.

In addition, most people are under the impression, as perpetuated by the Federal Deposit Insurance Corporation (FDIC), that their money is insured up to $250,000.[3] In theory, this is correct. However, as of September 30, 2007, the FDIC had $53 billion in insurance reserves, which represents only 1.22% of total insured deposits. That means that if one decent-size bank goes out of business, it could bankrupt the FDIC's current reserves. Now, this doesn't mean your money is not completely safe. When the FDIC runs out of money, which I believe it will very shortly, it will borrow money from the U.S. Treasury. There are many opinions on this matter, but several I have

---

3. The recent "bailout" that was passed in October 2008 increased the depositor coverage from $100,000 per account to $250,000 per account.

read believe the total FDIC shortfall will exceed $500 billion. In order to borrow the money, Congress will have to pass legislation that allows the FDIC to do so. Once again, it will be the U.S. taxpayers who front the money for this shortfall. I do not expect Congress to deny any such request, for it would likely lead to large-scale protests and riots. One advantage the FDIC has, however, is that because it is an insurance company, it can increase the insurance premiums on the remaining banks to pay back the loan to cover the shortfall.

If we do enter a Greater Depression, many more banks will go out of business. It is possible, although somewhat unlikely, that there will not be enough money to pay all insured depositors. The government will argue that it can always print more money, but we're relying on politicians to fix the problem, which is something I'm not confident about. If you look at the total money supply in the United States, only 3% is in printed currency. The rest exists as electronic money. If even a small percentage of the population demands its money back in currency, there would not be enough available to meet the demand. Bank runs —onslaughts of panicked customers trying to withdraw their deposits—were a feature of the Great Depression. Americans were shocked to discover that they couldn't get their money out as the banks went belly up. It is possible that this could happen again, so you should be prepared just in case.

The above analysis is our opinion on various investments based on what we have read and researched. We are not financial advisers, nor experts for that matter. Please do your own homework and invest wisely.

Conclusion

ongratulations! You've faced the music, dealt with a serious topic, and learned how to take the scariness out of the word *recession*. That wasn't too painful, was it? My hope is that you now know a little bit more about economics and have replaced fear and hopelessness with awareness and confidence.

One of the things I discovered while writing this book was that there is an immediate and serious need for support of the women who are suffering as a result of the recession. I urge you to visit my website, www.practicalchic.org, where we're building a forum for women to share their stories, support each other, share new money-saving ideas, and talk shop. There's no need to face this recession alone. We're all in the same boat. The emotional issues that come with a shaky economy are numerous, and I'm glad to provide a place online where people can go vent and help each other.

Acknowledgments

First, I must thank my amazing husband, Dan. Thank you for your humor, strength, and calm amidst chaos, and for being my rock. Thank you for finally convincing me that economics is actually exciting, and for preventing me from throwing this manuscript into the trash when I wanted to give up. You are a beautiful human being—in every way. I'm so glad we wrote this book together. When we're in our nineties we'll be looking back and laughing.

Thank you, Jessica, for always being there for us—this book would not have been possible without you. Dean, thank you for being *you*, and for keeping Dan out of trouble. Christian and Kelly, thanks for your never-ending encouragement. And Jan, you are a bright light. Just being around you makes me want to do great things.

Special thanks to Rachel Haimowitz (who edited the first version of this book), one of the smartest and funniest people I know, for keeping me out of trouble, slugging through this project with me, and who totally "got" my vision of making this subject funny. How did I get so lucky to find you?

I am so honored to be working with the talented crew at Atria Books, I'm still pinching myself. Judith Curr, thank you for taking my call. Special thanks to Sarah Durand, my editor, for being so supportive and facilitating this project at lightning speed.

Laura Dail, who is a total rock star, and really, a gift from heaven—I'm so glad you're my agent.

Rita Van Amber, who survived the Great Depression and generously let me use her Great Depression stories as excerpts in this book. Mel Bartholomew, the ASPO, and Michael Hodges for their charts and graphs. And of course the inspiration of Peter Schiff and Jim Rogers—thanks for sticking your necks out.

And lastly, thanks to the crooks on Wall Street, whose antics provided ample material for this book.

Resources

The following books, websites, and businesses have been a tremendous source of inspiration on a wide variety of topics. Though not comprehensive, this list includes some of my favorite resources and the ones I believe will help people the most.

MONEY AND PERSONAL FINANCE

Women and Money: Owning the Power to Control Your Destiny by Suze Orman (Spiegel & Grau, 2007).
TV show on CNBC is highly entertaining, and every once in a while she'll even suggest where to move your money.

STARTING AND OWNING A BUSINESS

The 4-Hour Workweek: Escape 9–5, Live Anywhere, and Join the New Rich by Timothy Ferriss (Crown, 2007).
Tim explains how you can live better by increasing your income and freedom—as well as by improving your enjoyment of life with the income you have.

CULTIVATING A STRONG MIND

Feminine Force: Release the Power Within You to Create the Life You Deserve by Georgette Mosbacher (Fireside, 1994).
Mosbacher is personally responsible motivating me to start my first company, at age nineteen. She is an inspiration to women and girls alike.

Think and Grow Rich!: The Original Version, Restored and Revised by Napoleon Hill (Aventine, 2004).
Originally printed in 1937, this landmark book discusses how changing your thoughts can improve your life—a concept recently made popular on *Oprah* and in other, newer books by Eckhard Tolle, Wayne Dyer, etc.

Pimsleur Language Programs. *www.pimsleur.com.* *1-800-831-5497.*

FAMILY

The Creative Family: How to Encourage Imagination and Nurture Family Connections by Amanda Blake Soule (Trumpeter, 2008).
I love Amanda's clever resourcefulness—a real asset during a recession. (224 pages)

Well-Behaved Children: 100 Tips from Parents Who Have Them by Devra E. Doiron (Seaview, 2000).
This clever little gem is not well known, but it should be. It succinctly shows the reader how to get children to cooperate and behave themselves. The approach is gentle and kind but gets results. (128 pages)

Money Doesn't Grow on Trees: A Parent's Guide to Raising Financially Responsible Children by Neale S. Godfrey and Carolina Edwards (Fireside, 2006).
It's never too early for financial literacy. Children need to be educated about money, and this book is a good place to start. (192 pages)

401 Ways to Get Your Kids to Work at Home by Bonnie Runyan McCullough and Susan Walker Monson (St. Martin's Griffin, 2003).
A great resource on implementing the working-family idea. (256 pages)

Last Child in the Woods: Saving Our Children From Nature-Deficit Disorder by Richard Louv (Algonquin, 2008).
A great message: kids need time outdoors, every day, whatever the weather. Make it happen. (390 pages)

SAVING MONEY, THRIFTING, AND DEBT

The Complete Tightwad Gazette by Amy Dacyczyn (Villard, 1998).

Amy Dacyczyn, the "frugal zealot," compiled and bound her popular newsletter, *The Tightwad Gazette*, into one hefty, information-packed book. Its ideas for saving money, recycling, and getting the best deal on everything are endless. I highly recommend it for surviving a weak economy. (959 pages)

Stories and Recipes of the Great Depression of the 1930's by Rita Van Amber. Van Amber Publishers, 862 E. Cecil St., Neenah, WI 54956, 920-722-8357 or 715-235-7702.

These stories are a real wake-up call for our generation, and I am grateful to have been given the permission to reprint some of them in this book. Thank you, Rita! (309 pages)

How to Get Out of Debt, Stay Out of Debt and Live Prosperously by Jerrold Mundis (Bantam, 2003).

Based on the principles of Debtors Anonymous, this book details the steps you should take to eliminate debt. (320 pages)

WEBSITES

www.overstock.com
www.amazon.com
www.ubid.com
www.dealsofamerica.com
www.dealtaker.com
www.froogle.com
www.pricegrabber.com

COOKING, HEALTH, AND FOOD

All New Square Foot Gardening by Mel Bartholomew. (Cool Springs, 2006).

Mel's method is simply the easiest way to grow large amounts of produce in a tiny area. It's fun, too! (272 pages) Also visit www.squarefootgardening.com.

Super Baby Food by Ruth Yaron (F. J. Roberts, 1998).
Everything you need to know about feeding children from ages 0–3 with
a strong emphasis on healthy (not processed) foods. Includes thousands of
money-saving and time-saving techniques. It's the bible of baby food. (608
pages).

*Don't Panic—Dinner's in the Freezer: Great-Tasting Meals You
Can Make Ahead* by Suzie Martinez, Vanda Howell, and Bonnie
Garcia (Revell, 2005).
This cookbook is dedicated to freezer meals and batch cooking. (240 pages)

How to Cook a Wolf by M. F. K. Fisher (Northpoint, 1988).
This foodie classic was written in the 1940s, when money was short and
food was rationed. M. F. K. Fisher's superb writing is surpassed only by her
sense of humor and uncommonly practical outlook. This book is for those
who love to eat elegantly and savor the experience of food, even during hard
economic times. (216 pages).

*Celebrate the Rain: Cooking with the Fresh and Abundant
Flavors of the Northwest* (Junior League of Seattle, 2004).
The number one cookbook in the Northwest and the follow-up to the
equally awesome *Simply Classic, Celebrate the Rain* is one of those well-loved
cookbooks that has food stains all over it. My copy is spotted and tattered
because the recipes are nothing short of incredible. The Five Bean Chili is
a family favorite (and it freezes beautifully), and all my friends beg for the
recipe. (272 pages)

*Eat to Live: The Revolutionary Formula for Fast and Sustained
Weight Loss* by Joel Fuhrman (Foreword by Dr. Mehmet Oz)
(Little, Brown, 2005)
This book is about maximizing nutrition and minimizing disease, especially
diabetes, cancer, and heart disease. Extremely well researched, this book will
shock, horrify, and awaken you to the proven correlation between diet and
disease prevention. Life changing—read it! (304 pages)

Skinny Bitch by Kim Barnouin and Rory Freedman (Running
Press, 2005).
Don't let the snotty title and cute cover fool you. This is a shocking vegan

manifesto that bullies the reader into eating healthier, one soy burger at a time. (224 pages)

Body for Life: 12 Weeks to Mental and Physical Strength by Bill Phillips and Michael D'Orso (Collins Living, 1999).
A guide for quick and effective workouts, old-school bodybuilder style. This book also showcases a diet that is pro-vegetable but heavy on protein. (201 pages)

WEBSITES

www.epicurious.com
www.cookinglight.com
www.allrecipes.com

ECONOMICS

The New Paradigm for Financial Markets: The Credit Crisis of 2008 and What It Means by George Soros (PublicAffairs, 2008).
Our credit-based economy is totally screwed up. George explains why, and where it's going. (208 pages)

Crash Proof: How to Profit from the Coming Economic Collapse by Peter D. Schiff (Wiley, 2007).
Peter provides a compelling and detailed analysis of what's happening in the U.S. economy right now, and how to protect yourself. An awesome read, even for non–econ geeks.

A Bull in China: Investing Profitably in the World's Greatest Market by Jim Rogers (Random House, 2008).
After founding Quantum Fund, Jim Rogers "retired" at age thirty-seven. His subsequent meanderings around the world and his passion for economics and finance make this a fun read about the Chinese economy and how you can fit into it. (240 pages)

Tomorrow's Gold: Asia's Age of Discovery by Marc Faber (CSLA, 2008).
Marc is very good at predicting economic events and timing investments for profit. (378 pages)

Twilight in the Desert: The Coming Saudi Oil Shock and the World Economy by Matthew R. Simmons (Wiley, 2006).

An expert on the oil industry, Simmons questions how much Saudi oil actually exists, and whether oil production is sustainable on a massive scale. He also discusses the increasing supply-demand problem for oil. (464 pages)

WEBSITES

www.lifeaftertheoilcrash.net
www.hsdent.com
www.europac.net
www.kitco.com

About the Authors

Jill Keto

An entrepreneur since the age of nineteen and lifelong crusader of a "Practical Chic" lifestyle, artist and jewelry designer. Jill Keto's work has been featured in Maxim, VH1, and other media, and is collected by celebrities. She is a stiletto-wearing do-it-yourself zealot (from car repair to pedicures), degreed mechanical engineer, mother of two, organic mini-farmer, and jazz musician.

Dan Keto

A graduate of the Harvard Business School Owner/President Management Program and the United States Naval Academy, practical economic theory guru and business owner Daniel Keto resides in the Seattle area. He is a marathon-running, nature-loving economics geek, spending his off hours either devouring financial news, or speaking to universities, Fortune 500 companies, and nonprofits.